THEN AND THERE SERIES
GENERAL EDITOR
MARJORIE REEVES

The Peasants' Revolt

MARY PRICE

Illustrated from contemporary sources

LONGMAN

LONGMAN GROUP LIMITED
London
*Associated companies, branches and representatives
throughout the world*

© Longman Group Ltd 1980
*All rights reserved. No part of this publication
may be reproduced, stored in a retrieval system,
or transmitted in any form or by any means, electronic,
mechanical, photocopying, recording or otherwise,
without the prior permission of the Copyright owner.*

First published 1980
ISBN 0 582 20164 0

Set in 11/12½ Baskerville, Monophoto 169

*Printed in Hong Kong by
Sheck Wah Tong Printing Press Ltd*

Common Ground Filmstrips

Medieval Life
A series of carefully reconstructed colour pictures
which convey the richness and variety of life in
medieval times. Suitable for ages 9–13.

The Castle
The Crusaders
The Knight
The Monastery
The Town
The Village

Contents

To the Reader

Nowadays we are used to marches and demonstrations. We see them on TV, filmed as they happen, eye-witnesses describe them, we may even watch them in our own town. We know that people who have grievances or complaints often draw attention to them by protests. Sometimes they are silent protests, sometimes noisy but harmless, sometimes they are violent and dangerous demonstrations.

This is the story of a protest made in England 600 years ago, a story of danger and death, of marches and riots which went on through the summer of 1381. A French writer, Jean Froissart, wrote an account of it, and his first words are 'In the youth of King Richard there fell on England great mischief and rebellion, by which deed England was all but lost'. We now call this 'great mischief and rebellion' the Peasants' Revolt.

Our modern ways of broadcasting news are so quick and clear that we can actually see the faces, and hear the shouts of protesters and marchers, and read what is written on their placards and banners. Even so, it is often rather difficult to discover exactly who they are, what the protests are about and whether there are any results. In the case of a protest made hundreds of years ago it is of course very difficult indeed. For example, how do we know that Froissart's story is accurate? He was not even in England in 1381 so he could not have seen the Peasants' Revolt himself, and when he wrote he must have relied on what other people told him. We have to try to check the truth of what he says. Fortunately other men also wrote histories of those far-off events. Their writings are called *chronicles*. One of the best is by Thomas Walsingham, a monk who worked in the *scriptorium* of St Albans Abbey, and there are others which you will find mentioned on page 89 in the section called 'How do we know?'

Words printed in *italics* are explained in the Glossary on page 94.

1 A Boy King and a Discontented Land

'Woe to you, O land, when your king is a child.' These words come from the Old Testament of the Bible and people have often remembered them when a sovereign was too young and weak to govern his kingdom properly. They must have been murmured by many people in England when Richard II became king in 1377, for he was only ten years old and his throne was not likely to be a comfortable one. He was the son of Edward, the Black Prince, but his father had died in 1376 and so Richard actually followed his grandfather Edward III

The Black Prince, in full armour. This figure is in Canterbury Cathedral

(1327–77), once called 'the most famous knight of his day, glorious among the great ones of the world'. But the last years of both his grandfather and his father were far from glorious.

Edward III at the end of his reign was feeble with age and wandering in his mind – a great change from his younger days when he 'raged like a boar in the thick of the fight' carrying his shield with a white swan painted on it, shouting as a battle cry, 'Hey, hey, the White Swan. In God's name I am your man.' The Black Prince was ill for five years before he died, so ill that at last he could not even mount his horse and had to be carried everywhere in a *litter*, – a sad thing for a famous fighting man. People thought that both father and son were perfect examples of knighthood, brave in battle, generous to their enemies (if they were important enough!), splendidly armed and magnificently horsed. Both of them loved 'the bloody battle, the glory and the *loot*', of war, and both had their fill of war, which was the favourite sport of kings, princes and nobles in the Middle Ages. During their lives they performed some fair deeds, but many black ones as well.

England was at war with France off and on, all through the reign of Edward III, in a long-drawn-out struggle called

Soldiers looting a town. They are drinking, stealing all they want, and destroying the rest: smashing jugs and trampling on hats

the Hundred Years War. Most of the battles were fought in France and the land there was mercilessly laid waste. Both the King and the Prince allowed the English armies to rob and plunder almost at will; it was all part of the sport and it was a good way of keeping soldiers happy when money for their pay ran out. 'Barns full of corn, houses full of riches, carts, horses, swine, muttons and other beasts' they seized. These cruel results of war were taken as a matter of course by most people. Certainly the knightly leaders thought nothing of them. Plunder and loot were what a true knight deserved, and every well-born boy hoped to be one.

Young Richard must have been taught from the very first that, before all else, he must be a true knight like his father and grandfather, brave, courteous, skilful on a horse and with a sword and lance, always ready for a fight. You can see his royal seal, with which all important *documents* had to be stamped, below. On one side it shows the King in state on his throne, on the other, a fully armed knight on a prancing horse, a picture of what Richard probably hoped to be but never was – glorious, powerful and admired.

It was not that he was a weakling. We know from his skeleton

The Great Seal of England, made for Richard II

7

that he was over 1.8 metres tall and straight of limb, 'full active in limb and *lithe*', as one poet wrote about him. He was not a coward either for he could show great courage in dangerous moments as you will hear later. He was simply not cut out to be a fighting man in the same way that his ancestors were. He was often rather lazy and impatient, not the kind of person to enjoy long boring hours of practice, sweating inside heavy armour, and learning to use weapons on horseback, all thought necessary in the education of a prince. Instead he was interested in quite different things. He liked books and pictures, especially if they were portraits of himself for he was proud of his good looks, the thick golden hair and fair skin of his *Plantagenet* family. He kept his books carefully in his private chamber, but they were not just for show. Froissart says that he could read French easily and we know his books must have been well used for they had to be re-covered at intervals. Among his bills was one for rebinding nineteen of them in red or blue-and-white satin, with blue silk markers and gold clasps. Writers were always delighted when the King accepted one of their books. One writer, John Gower, who was sometimes very critical of Richard, was so pleased that he wrote in the front 'A boke for King Richard's sake. To whome belongeth my *allegiance* and all mine heart's obedience.'

Richard was also keenly interested in clothes, the finer the better, and the royal tailor must have been a busy and important man, constantly turning out new coats and *mantles* for the King in rich silks and cloth of gold, embroidered with precious stones. One coat was of cloth of gold on a green ground, buttoned with little bells of gold and embroidered with large pearls round the collar and sleeves. It is not surprising that one of those coats cost over £1000 and that courtiers who liked to copy the King's clothes often wore their whole fortunes on their backs! One of his friends had eight fur cloaks, and a white leather coat with fifty-four gold buttons.

Besides fine clothes Richard enjoyed good food, and the court cookery book, written by his master-cooks, still exists. It is called 'The Forme of Cury' (cookery) and has recipes of all the dishes most popular at the royal table, some of which must have been delicious, such as mulberries in honey, but others which sound rather peculiar, such as minced pheasant mixed with wine, ginger, cinnamon, cloves and about a kilogram of sugar! The cooks say at the beginning of the book that 'it teaches a man for to make common *potages* and common meats, *craftily* and wholesomely, and also curious potages and meats, and *solitées* for all manner of men, high and low.' One example of a common potage was this: 'Take beans and dry them in an oven and *hull* them well and *winnow* out the *husk* and wash them. When they are clene, seethe in good broth and ete with bacon.' This would have been very suitable for poor folk but a solitée would not, for it was a sweet pudding made of paste, wax and sugar, and sugar was very expensive. Here is another recipe which you can put into modern English if you use the list of words at the back of the book. 'Take a *pottel* of greke wyne, or *renyshe* wyne. Take honey, flower of ryce, powder of gynger, sugar of cinnamon, and mulberry and *meddle* all this together. Boyle it, salt it, and look that it be standing (cool).'

There is no doubt that Richard was very extravagant and many grumbled at his waste of money and mocked his new-fangled ways, for example, his strange habit of blowing his nose on a wisp of fine silk instead of wiping it on his sleeve or on the back of his hand as most people did. He is said to have been the first Englishman to use a handkerchief! As he grew up his extravagance increased and so did his pride. Sometimes he would sit in state for hours as you see him on page 10 and when he looked at a man, that man had to bend his knee. His pride, his love of luxury, gradually set many people against him. Yet those who saw him crowned with magnificent ceremony at Westminster in 1377, a small solemn boy almost weighed down by his royal robe embroidered with golden eagles, wearing a sword and spurs, and holding the sceptre and the orb, hoped that when he was a man he might be the saviour of England, and that 'joyful and blyssed thynges' lay ahead.

9

'An *ympe* begins for to growe,' they said 'that shall hold his foemen under foot.'

Richard himself was so tired after his coronation that one of his knights had to carry him home.

A saviour was certainly needed, for much was wrong in England. The war with France still dragged on, but for ten years there had been no glorious victories like the battles of Crécy and Poitiers, only defeats and loss of land. The expense of keeping armies in France was terribly high, even though soldiers were seldom paid, and the King's ministers were for ever demanding more money, which was poured out with no results. Even the shores of England were not safe from French pirates, who sailed boldly along the south coast and landed where they liked to raid and rob. They attacked Hastings and Rye, and once they seized the Isle of Wight for a time. London itself was not safe from them. In 1377 the Mayor and aldermen of London were so worried about the perils from the French that they discussed the matter with 200 wealthy men of the city. They decided to set a watch 'every day and night from noon to noon with at least 100 men-at-arms, in case the enemy should come to set fire to the shipping in the Thames and invade the city'. They also stretched an iron chain across the river to hold back enemy ships. It never seemed to dawn on the government that it would be sensible to pull out of the war and end the waste of men and money. The country went on fighting it out with the French, always dreaming of old victories and hoping for new ones.

Yet nearly every one at heart was discontented. The King's ministers were bitterly criticised, even called traitors, and they did not enjoy it. The soldiers hated being beaten and wanted regular pay. The tax-payers grumbled furiously at each new demand for money. 'Tax hath ruined us alle', they

Opposite: *Richard II, painted in 1381 when he was fourteen. He still looks very young and rather lost, so his courage in facing the rebels was all the more remarkable. Notice the robes of state, the crown, sceptre and orb*

said and in Parliament some men declared plainly that 'the *commons* are too poor and feeble to endure fresh taxes'. All Englishmen, except the most obstinate and stupid, must have felt anger and dismay: ministers and nobles; soldiers and churchmen both high and low; plain merchants and tradesmen; the wealthy and the not so wealthy. And right at the bottom of the heap were those who suffered most: the poor men; the peasants in the villages and the lowest townsmen in their horrible slums; the people who had never yet spoken out in such a way as to frighten the great and powerful ones of the land. They were now about to do so and the result was a rebellion which shook England from end to end, 'an uproar of the whole kingdom'.

The uproar first broke out over the poll tax. 'Poll' means 'head', so a poll tax was one which fell on every head, or person, in the land. It was one of the ways by which the King's ministers raised money for the war and in the autumn of 1380 money was again urgently needed. The royal treasury was nearly empty and Parliament had to be asked again to agree to new taxes. So in November the Lords and Commons were called to meet at Northampton, well away from London, where the people were in a very restive mood. It was a miserably wet autumn, so wet that many members of Parliament, met such '*outrageous* floods that they could scarce ride through the water'. When they arrived at Northampton, some of them three days late, and in a bad temper, they were even more annoyed to find there were not enough lodgings in the little town, not enough food for themselves and their tired horses. They then had to listen to the Chancellor's story and there was little comfort in what they heard. The Chancellor was the Archbishop of Canterbury, Simon Sudbury, a good honest man, but not clever in money matters. He and the Treasurer, Sir Robert Hales, had to admit that their sums had gone hopelessly wrong. They had been forced to borrow on all sides. Even the King's jewels had been pawned, including two coronets of gold set with pearls and other precious stones, and 'one sword for Parliament, set with diamonds, rubies, sapphires and pearls'. In spite of this, three months' pay was still owing to the English armies in France. Parliament grumbled long and loud, for it seemed to them 'that money had been badly and deceitfully used and nothing done for the profit of the realm', and they were right. But still they did not demand an end to the war. Instead 'for the safety of the kingdom and the keeping of the sea' they agreed to a new poll tax.

Groats and half groats made in Richard II's reign

It was the third in three years, the heaviest, and the most unfair. It was pushed up from one *groat* per head (about five pence) to three and was to be paid by every person of fifteen and over, except widows and genuine beggars. Five pence sounds a very small sum to us, but we must remember that very little money went into a poor man's pocket in 1380. A groat was about a week's wages so it would take at least three weeks for one person to pay his poll tax. If there were people in a family who were over fifteen, but getting no wages, the head of the family had to pay their poll tax too. There was a rather vague suggestion that the rich should pay more than their share, so that the poor paid less, but as you can imagine, not many rich people would do this unless they were forced. Anyhow in many places there were no rich people at all. If, for instance, you lived in Brockley, Suffolk, you were very lucky, for there was a knight in that village who paid 30p for himself and 30p for his wife, and five prosperous 13 farmers who paid 15p each, so that the poor got off with 2p or 3p. But the nearby village of Chevington had no resident lord and only one well-to-do farmer and all the seventy-eight villagers had to pay the tax in full. Such unfairness was bound to cause trouble.

The collectors of poll tax began their work at once and went on with it all through December, January and February, the dark months when food ran short in many homes, and the cold bit into the very bones of hungry men. Many of them must have been just like the ploughman described by William Langland in 'Piers Plowman', hanging on to the handles of his plough in the winter fields, 'whose coat was of coarse stuff, his hood full of holes so that his hair stuck out of it, and as he trod the soil his toes peered out of his worn boots'. Such men, going home at sunset to a dark leaky cottage, and a family famished with hunger, supping on a coarse loaf of beans and bran, yesterday's vegetables, and a bit of bacon, must have wondered desperately what they could do to find the tax money. One man said: 'The tax-collector comes with great threats...bristling like a boar, and says he means to strip my home quite bare.'

What could they do? A way out seems to have occurred to people all over England, and that was to give the tax-collectors false facts about the size and ages of their families.

William Langland must have seen many ploughmen like this one, guiding a heavy plough behind oxen plodding slowly along – an unpleasant job in cold, rainy weather

Some declared, perhaps, that a son who was very small for his age was not yet fifteen. Many simply hid one or two of the family in the woods, usually women, an aunt perhaps, or a couple of daughters. Not surprisingly tax-collectors throughout the country reported that they found it exceedingly difficult to discover the names of those who ought to be paying the tax, and that the money came in slowly and in small amounts. When the tax lists were carefully examined and compared, a very queer thing seemed to have happened. If the lists were correct, then in three years there had been a huge fall in the grown-up population of England, and about one in every three people had simply disappeared, although there had been no outbreak of plague, no famine, no extraordinary disaster. There was also a strange shortage of women in many places! It soon dawned on the government that they were being cheated and they acted swiftly. Royal officials were sent riding out in haste from London with orders to look into the numbers of all persons who were aged fifteen and upwards, to find out who had sent in false lists, and to 'seize and arrest those acting against the king's command'. These were the collectors who bristled like boars! The tax was to be paid at once and all the money must be in the treasury by April. By May the south-east of England, which the officials reached first, was on the verge of revolt.

2 Rebellious Subjects

At the very beginning of Richard II's reign, the English poet John Gower had foretold in one of his poems that something unpleasant would happen before long, and that all would feel it as one feels the sting of a nettle. To him the 'nettle' was the mass of the common people whom he despised but feared, and his fore-telling came true.

The nettle first began to sting in a small village in Essex called Fobbing (see the map opposite). The royal official appointed to collect all the unpaid poll tax in that county was Thomas Bampton, who was considered 'a great lord in that country because of his great state'. On 1 June 1381 he began his work. He had three clerks and two of the King's *sergeants-at-arms* to help him and among the first people he summoned were men from Fobbing. Fobbing is about 48 kilometres from London, not far from the river Thames. Now it is almost swallowed up in houses, shops and oil tanks, but in 1381 it was in the depths of the country. The people were farmers and fishermen and they held their land as tenants from the Abbess of Barking Abbey. There were deep woods round the village where they drove their pigs to feed, and between the village and the Thames was flat marshland which, though dismal and wet in winter, gave plenty of sweet grass for sheep in summer. Also, as far back as men could remember, the villagers had had fishing rights in the river and the many *creeks* which ran through the marshes.

Thomas Bampton's visit was probably expected, for news from London could travel fairly quickly into nearby places, and evidently the men of Fobbing, led by John Baker (so-called

16

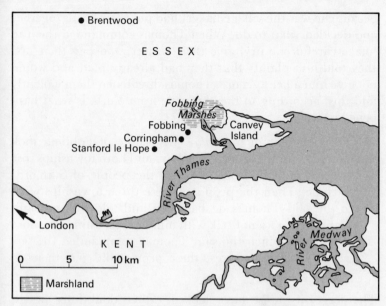

You can see in this map how near to each other Fobbing, Corringham and Stanford-le Hope were, and also how close all three were to the Thames. The creeks round Canvey Island were two of the ones where Fobbing men could fish

The men of Fobbing would use boats like this – not always so crowded! There were plenty of fish in the Thames, including salmon, as it was not as polluted as it is now

because he was the village baker) had put their heads together and decided what to do. When Thomas commanded them to 'make careful enquiry, give their answer, and pay their tax' they told him plainly that they had already paid and would not give him a penny more. Thomas threatened them violently and this, according to the chronicle from York, is what happened next:

> Then for fear of his *malice* the people of Fobbing took counsel with those of Corringham and both townships rose and assembled...together with the people of Stanford-le-Hope. Then the people of these three townships went to the said Thomas de Bampton and told him outright that they would not talk with him, nor give him any more money. At which the said Thomas commanded the sergeants-at-arms to arrest these people and put them in prison

The sergeants must have looked rather doubtfully at the sullen villagers standing there and wondered how they could arrest them all. The men of the three townships looked back. Then suddenly they fell upon Thomas, his clerks and the sergeants, beat them and stoned them and sent them flying along the road back to London.

It was a bold and dangerous thing to do and the villagers, now in even greater fear of malice, rapidly made for the woods and hid. They hid there until they were almost starving, but they did not waste their time. Instead they sent messengers about the countryside to stir up other villages to join them. Some of the messengers must have walked or ridden to London for London men were among those who came to help. We know the names of two of the first to arrive. They were butchers, called Thomas Attwell and Roger Harvey, which showed that the country people were not alone in their protest, or in the deep resentment which made thousands of them leave their families and homes, and their urgent work of sheep-shearing, hay-making and fishing, to defy the law of the land.

18   They were not a great danger to anyone at this point.

Ignorant, and shabby, and dressed in shapeless garments made of rough grey wool, '*hodden* grey' it was called, they could not have looked very frightening for 'some only carried sticks, some swords covered with rust, some merely axes and others bows – reddened with age and smoke; many had arrows with only one plume. It was difficult to find one man that was properly armed.' A small troop of well-armed soldiers could have scattered them to the four winds, but this is exactly what no one thought of sending into Essex. Instead another royal official arrived, with a handful of clerks and no armed escort at all, whereupon the common people rose against him too and frightened him so much that 'he travelled home as quickly as possible in fear of his life'.

Up to that moment the rebels had stopped short of killing and had done no great damage, but now their mood changed. To watch royal officers turn tail and run was a pleasant sight and it tempted them to go further. They seized three of the harmless clerks, beheaded them, stuck the heads on poles and carried them through the villages. They hunted down all who had given information to the King's men about false tax returns, or who had betrayed the ringleaders of the revolt, and killed them too and 'threw down their houses'. They swore they would do the same to all the lawyers and royal servants they could find and *rampaged* through the country in search of them. Clearly they meant what they said, for later they marched to the home of Sir Robert Hales, Treasurer of England, at Cressing Temple and 'a very fine and pleasant manor'. Sir Robert was just coming there on a visit and had ordered his servants to lay in stocks of food and wine. The rebels broke in, ate all the food (for they were nearly always hungry) drank three casks of fine wine and burnt the whole place to the ground. At this show of violence all the great lords and well-known people fled towards London or any other part where they would be safe.

You would expect that when an unruly mob twice defied the King's officials, murdered royal servants and destroyed the home of a great officer of the crown, the government would act quickly to punish them. Nothing of the kind happened. Richard II was still only a boy of fourteen, and not likely to know what to do, but he had round him a Council of experienced ministers, and powerful grown-up relations, among them three uncles who were well-known soldiers. However, instead of taking a firm line, these men seem to have become helpless with fear and confusion. Every day the troubles grew, every day news reached them of growing numbers of rebels in Essex, to the east of London, and of riotous bands of men moving in Kent to the south and they knew only too well that there were many in London who would gladly follow them if a chance came. It really seemed to the Council that the very ground of England was shaking under their feet.

While they dithered and hesitated a band of the Kentish rebels rowed across the Thames and consulted with the Essex men on the other side. On 4 June they took about a hundred of them back to join forces with those on the south bank, while most of the Essex rebels moved towards London. In the next chapter we shall follow both groups but first we must try to find out why this rebellion, which began among a few hundred poor and ignorant people, spread so far and so fast.

All that had happened so far was that three small villages had got into trouble with the tax-collectors, which does not seem enough to frighten the King's ministers and send people flying for safety, nor, as you will hear, to cause London to be invaded by 50,000 rebels and even to put the King's life in danger. Why did this unimportant event grow into 'a great mischief and rebellion'? What lay behind it all?

Some of the *chroniclers* thought they knew, but you must remember that they were all shocked by the revolt and very much against the rebels, so that they show little sympathy for their grievances. They refer to them as 'enemies of our Lord the King' and 'this wicked mob'; they speak of them as being like 'the most rabid dogs' and 'drunken pigs'. Thomas Walsingham showed his contempt when he wrote that the men of Essex were '5,000 of the most mean commons and rustics'. He thought the rebels were possessed by devils and that the revolt was a punishment for England's sins. Froissart said it happened 'all because of the ease and riches that the common people were of, which moved them to rebellion' to get even more. But the reasons for the revolt were much more complicated than either Walsingham or Froissart thought, and we must try to find them.

You can make a list of three causes of discontent from chapter one. These were: the hopeless and expensive war with France; the inefficient and unpopular ministers; and, of course, the poll tax. But there were other deeper grievances which had smouldered away for many years. In 1381, sparked off by the poll tax, they burst into flame. Chief of these was an old, old quarrel between lords (the masters) and their tenants (workers), chiefly in the country, but growing in towns too. If you have read some of the other Then and There books about how people lived in medieval times you will already know something about this quarrel. For instance, you may have discovered that people were roughly divided into three main classes, sometimes described as the men who prayed (abbots, bishops, monks and priests), the men who fought (kings, princes, nobles and knights), and the men who worked (chiefly peasants but also craftsmen). These classes are neatly illustrated on page 22 by the picture of a medieval king dreaming, not very happily, about his subjects.

Almost all the land of England belonged to the first two classes, and their wealth came from it in the shape of food crops and animals. All this wealth was produced by the hard unending toil of the third class, many of whom were *villeins*. The mark of a villein was that he was not free. He was bound to his lord, and was obliged to give service (work) on the lord's land for so many days each week, and extra at specially busy times. In return he got a house (of a sort) and a piece of land on which to grow food for himself and his family. If by any chance he and his wife managed to grow a bit more than they needed, and they lived near a market town, they could sell this extra and make a little money. The arrangement was a kind of bargain between lords and tenants, but the lords had

A King's nightmare. He is dreaming uneasily about the three sections of his subjects, men who pray or fight or work. All are demanding something from him

much the best of it and most tenants knew it. As well as service from their tenants the lords also had the right to take what were known as dues, such as extra eggs at Easter, firewood collected at Christmas, and bundles of the tenant's own straw for the horses at harvest time. When a man died, the lord took more dues, the best beast, the best tools, the best coat, or a sum of money called a 'heriot', before the dead man's heir could take over the house and land. All these services and dues were fixed by ancient customs and written down in manor records, and this is why, during the revolt, the rebels burnt all the manor records and papers they could find so that they could never be held bound by them again.

In the village of Broughton in Huntingdonshire the records were very carefully kept. One of the villeins there was Thomas, son of Henry. Thomas had to give seven different kinds of dues to his lord. Among them were a *bushel* of corn and a hen at Christmas and ten eggs at Easter. At acorn time he had to pay two pence for every full-grown pig he sent to feed in the woods, and one penny for every young one. But the worst burden for Thomas was the amount of work he had to do on the lord's land. For ten months of the year, from October to August, he had to work all day on Mondays, Tuesdays and Wednesdays. In August and September he had to work every day,

Men and women worked in the fields. Here the woman looks as if she is thinking about all the other things she has to do: cooking, cleaning, milking, and washing clothes for the household

except Sunday, 'from morning till night' at anything the lord demanded, 'and his wife with him'. You can imagine how very glad Thomas would be to see this record torn up and burnt!

As you can imagine a villein was nearly always poor. He had to spend a great deal of his time working for his lord, often just when he wanted to attend to his own crops. Poverty is hard to bear but what was much harder for many Englishmen was the fact that they were not free. If they were villeins they were forced to do service and pay dues. They were not free to leave the village and go to live and work elsewhere. They were not free to marry or let their sons and daughters marry without getting the lord's permission and paying yet another due. There were many other ways in which people were kept, as Froissart wrote, 'in great bondage'. They could even be given away by the lord. In 1358, Geoffrey, abbot of Selby in Yorkshire, gave away John, son of William de Stonesworth 'with all his *brood* and *chattels*', to one of his friends. What would you have felt like if you had been John or his wife or any of his brood?

This hateful lack of freedom caused great bitterness between lords and tenants. Long before the Peasants' Revolt people were complaining and trying to get free. Some ran away, perhaps to the wars, perhaps to a town, where they tried to remain hidden for a year and a day. After that the lord had no power to bring them back. Others just worked as badly as possible, or refused to work at all, but they could be severely punished for this and dared not do it too often. In 1377 Henry Jordan of Coleshill in Berkshire, was fined for refusing to work for his lord at harvest, and cutting his own little patch of corn instead. His brother, Thomas, went to the cornfield and disturbed the other villeins who were doing their service properly. He was fined too. Then there were endless complaints about unfair *stewards*. The men of Bocking in Essex hated the steward, John le Doo, and begged their lord to restrain him. They said that 'of his own conceit', he had increased their services 'two-fold, even three-fold, against all reason, and comes and demands services they are not bound to render [give]'.

The Lord's steward keeps his eye on tenants at work. He is ready to hit those he thought were lazy or surly

You can imagine how these grievances would mount up over the years, even though in some places there were changes for the better. Gradually some lords had freed their tenants. They found it much better to pay wages for work and take rent for houses and land, than to demand work and dues and face sullen men doing bad work or trying to escape from the village. But this did not heal the quarrel. For one thing the changes came very slowly and unevenly. One lord might free his tenants, but another in a nearby village would refuse to change, and kept his tenants unfree and bound to do his will. Such lords often found their tenants disappearing and angrily sought to bring them back. You will read about one of these in the next chapter. Also, when wages were paid there was the question of how much they were to be, and we know well how much trouble is caused today by arguments over wages. Of course the lords wanted to get people to work for them as cheaply as possible and of course the workers wanted to get as much money as they could. So the discontent went on and grew greater rather than less.

Then came the Black Death, that terrible outbreak of plague which appeared in Sicily in 1347 and reached England a

Mass burial of victims of the Black Death

year later. It spread like a forest fire, and for more than two years raged through the land, attacking old and young, rich and poor, village and town alike. Plague was nothing new in the fourteenth century but this outbreak travelled so fast and killed so horribly that it was given its own terrible name of the Black Death. In England one out of every three people died so that the population which was about 4½ million before it came had dropped by a million when the plague died away. You can read more about the Black Death in another Then and There book called 'The Black Death'.

The Black Death added to the discontents and it is not difficult to discover why. If you look at some of the places where it struck you can quickly spot some of the problems. Take Haddiscoe, a village in Norfolk. Here seventy people died of the plague and twenty-four of them left no living soul to inherit their homes and land which lay desolate. At another small place, Little Cornard in Essex, fifty tenants held land from the lord of the manor in March 1349. By November of that year twenty-one families had been completely wiped out – sixty people in all, and there were twenty empty houses and holdings of land. Only one new tenant had been found. There were hundreds more villages like this which in a few short months became silent and almost empty. Ask yourself what would happen in such places? If you were the lord what would you do with the empty fields getting more weedy and overgrown every day, with few or no people to work, and with no rents coming in? And if you were a tenant, what would you do when you realised that there were now very few of you and the lords were in urgent need of your labour?

Some lords simply gave up trying to get the fields ploughed and sown, and the crops gathered, and turned over to sheep-farming because a big flock could be looked after by one shepherd and his dog. Some tried to go back to the past and forced people to give them all the old services and dues, which caused great anger. On the other hand some who had not yet freed their villeins did so now, and hoped by this to persuade them to work on their land for wages. But whatever the lords did, they were left with the problem of how high wages were to be. It is no wonder that the 'labourers were so proud and lifted up that if anyone wished to have them he had to give them what they wanted'.

Then Parliament stepped in and tried to solve the problem by passing laws to say what wages were to be paid. These laws were called the Statutes of Labourers. There were two of them, passed in 1349 and 1351. If you read a few extracts from them you seem to hear the voices of irritated lords and masters very loud and clear, because they were the men who sat in Parliament, but you do not hear the grievances of the labourers. The first Statute began by saying that it was being passed 'because a great number of people have died of pestilence [plague], many men will not serve unless they receive very high wages', and the second spoke of 'men who are idle and unwilling to work without outrageous wages, double and treble of what they were wont to have'.

Both Statutes were on the side of the landlords. They ordered that wages were to be frozen at the amounts paid before the Black Death, not only the wages of workers on the land, like ploughmen, carters, shepherds and swineherds, but 27 also those of craftsmen, like tilers, carpenters, tanners and tailors. So lords and masters were to get labour on their land or in their workshops as cheaply as possible, and anyone who demanded more could be put in prison, or in the stocks, or even branded with a hot iron. It is not surprising that 'the labourers cursed the King and all his justices for making such laws to grieve them'. And it is really not surprising, with all these troubles, that when the poll tax fell on them it seemed to the common people of England a new and almost unbearable burden, and suddenly 'they refused to bear such injuries any longer'. All over England trouble broke out, beginning in Essex and Kent.

3 London Besieged

When the hundred Essex men rowed across to the south bank of the Thames on 4 June they found plenty of excitement there. As in Essex the revolt had flared up over the poll tax, and in Kent too, just as at Fobbing, a collector of taxes, Sir John Legge, who went to round up non-payers, was forced by threatening crowds to hurry back to London. Soon Kent was alive with noisy bands of peasants moving from place to place urging others to join them but with no very clear idea of what they were going to do. The Essex men joined a group of them led by Abel Ker and went with him to Dartford, collecting recruits as they went. Soon they formed a very large disorderly crowd, ready for real violence if something provoked them. This came almost at once and from one of those very lords, mentioned in chapter 2, who were still trying to keep the peasants in bondage as villeins. He was Sir Simon Burley, the knight of the royal household who had carried the ten-year-old King Richard II back to the palace of Westminster after the coronation, when he was too tired to walk or ride. He was a great friend of the King and a very rich man. When he died his will gave a list of his clothes and other goods. He left seven *tabards*, one of scarlet, embroidered in gold, and another cloth of gold lined with green silk, and forty-three pieces of armour, among them helmets, breast-plates and gloves.

Sir Simon was very unpopular among the common people in Kent, and he had just tracked down a certain John Belling who was living quietly in Gravesend (see map on page 31) and had claimed him as an escaped villein of his. The people of Gravesend thought well of John and had dared to go to Sir

Rochester Castle as it is today. This is where Simon Burley imprisoned John Belling

Simon, to say that he was 'a Christian and a man of good name'. They asked the knight to let John buy his freedom, but although he was rich he demanded £300 for this, a sum so large that he must have known quite well that no simple workman could possibly pay it. The townspeople protested and then Sir Simon 'grew angry and irritable, and out of the haughtiness of his heart' he seized John Belling and shut him up in Rochester castle. This was exactly what was needed to spark off violence, a proud and merciless lord determined to keep a man in bondage, and sure enough it did. Furiously angry and now with a clear aim before them, the rebels decided to go to Rochester and get John Belling out of prison. Yet, angry as they were, they did not, in the heat of the moment, lose their common sense for they also decided that men who lived within twelve leagues (50 kilometres) of the sea must go home and stay there 'to keep the sea-coasts free from enemies'. You already know who those enemies were likely to be. The rest marched to Rochester and attacked the great stone castle which for nearly 300 years had frowned over the town.

At first the knight in charge, Sir John Newton, defended it stoutly, but then, 'in fear of so great a multitude and seeing those people in fury and ready to slay him', he gave in and handed over the keys of the castle. The rebels swarmed in and led out John Belling and all the other prisoners in triumph. 'Then the men of Gravesend returned home with their companion [John] in great joy and without doing anything more.'

Others, however, were not so easily satisfied as the men of Gravesend and these did not go home. Instead they moved on to Maidstone and there on 7 June they chose a new leader: Wat Tyler. Up to now first one man and then another had come to the front in Essex and in Kent. We read their names perhaps once or twice in the chronicles, but none had lasted for more than a few days, or even a few hours. Now the commons chose a leader whose name appears in all the chronicles and in every book written about the Peasants' Revolt. The strange thing is that, though his name is famous, we really know very little about Wat Tyler and he remains a mystery

This map shows the main places where the rebels collected in Kent. You can trace their movements from place to place

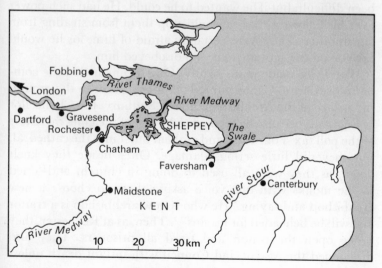

to this day. We do not know what he looked like, or exactly what he was or where he came from. He probably lived in Maidstone. He may have been a craftsman – a *tiler* of houses – he may have been a soldier back from the French wars, he may have been, as one chronicler calls him 'le plus grand robbare [the greatest robber]'. Some things about him are quite clear, enough to build up a kind of picture of the man.

Wat Tyler knew how to command men and make them obey his slightest word, for he quickly gained an extraordinary hold over thousands of ignorant and reckless rebels. In a few days they were so solidly behind him that his fiery energy drove them to march the 110 kilometres from Canterbury to London in two days. He was cunning, bold, insolent and merciless, as you will discover as you read on. He probably had dreams of glory and power, perhaps even of the crown itself. He often boasted that he would go anywhere at the head of 40,000 men, and 'shave the beards of all who dared to oppose him'. This meant that he would cut off their heads! Anyone who disobeyed him was quickly and savagely punished. He did not always try to stop the burning of houses and wild destruction of property, perhaps even for him that would have been difficult, but if he wanted to he could. He had such power over his followers that he could stop them from stealing from one another. They were certainly afraid of him, for he would execute on the spot anyone who disobeyed him.

Wat Tyler made plans swiftly. On 10 June he led the commons of Kent to Canterbury. There they burnt to the ground the palace of the Archbishop, Simon Sudbury, the Chancellor of England, because he seemed to be one of the chief inventors of the poll tax. Four thousand of them burst into the cathedral, but they did little serious damage. Once inside they knelt down, as they were all used to doing in church, and 'cried to the monks with one voice asking them to choose a new archbishop and saying "He who is now archbishop is a traitor and will be beheaded for his sins"'. Then, as at Rochester, they broke open the prison and freed all prisoners. They also threatened the Mayor and Council with instant death unless they swore 'to be faithful and loyal to King Richard and the loyal commons of England'. Of course, the frightened men did so at once. After this Wat Tyler departed with the main body of rebels towards London, leaving the rest behind to join up with disorderly citizens who quickly came out onto the streets of Canterbury, glad of a chance to loot and burn, and generally pay off old grudges against people they disliked. For instance, three men were dragged from their homes and killed for no crimes except that they were unpopular with the mob who cried out that they were traitors.

This kind of violence was breaking out all over Kent and Essex and in other parts as well. It seems senseless, but from the actions of the mobs you can discover what they were seeking. First, they sought revenge on men who had put burdens on them or who had anything to do with the poll tax. These men almost always had their houses 'cast down and burnt' and 'their horses, cows, sheep, pigs and all sorts of corn' either sold or stolen. The rebels were always in need of food, for most of them must have left home with only a loaf of coarse bread made chiefly of beans and bran, and a bit of bacon or cheese; few had money to buy more so they took what they could. Secondly, the rebels wanted to rescue prisoners, so they broke open gaols and freed captives. Thirdly, and perhaps more than anything else, they wanted to destroy every scrap of proof of unfreeness, service and dues, so they attacked lawyers and burnt all their papers and documents, some of which would now tell us much about our history but are lost for ever. Yet although in all these ways the rebels did damage, and stole, and knocked some people about, they killed very few, and until they got to London showed little desire for murder. And always (whatever treachery might be going on in Wat Tyler's mind), they showed complete loyalty to the King, and a touching belief that if only they could meet him face to face and tell him their troubles, he would 'amend' their lives.

Meanwhile the main body of rebels tramped along the rough dusty roads to London. On the way they met travellers 33 of various kinds, some simply going about their usual business; some, dismayed by what they heard and saw, hurrying for safety. Among these was a band of armed men escorting a frightened lady of high rank who was returning from a *pilgrimage* to the holy places of Kent. The crowd jostled her guard, and shouted rude jokes at her women, but they did not swear or jeer at her, only stared with curiosity and awe. She was the Princess of Wales, the King's mother, well known as beautiful, gentle and peace-loving, and the commons had no grudge against her.

Twice on their journey a royal messenger arrived from the King himself. The first demanded to know why they were behaving in such a fashion and 'for what cause they were making insurrection in the land'. The commons sent back to say they had risen to deliver him from the traitors that were round him. Then the King sent again, 'bidding them cease their doings in reverence to him, till he could speak with them'. They answered that they wished to see him and speak with him at Blackheath and marched on.

One of their companions on this journey was a man whom they treated with great respect. This was John Ball 'the crazy priest of Kent' and, after Wat Tyler, the most important person in the revolt, for he put into words all the hopes and longings which had brought it about. He was already well known to many people, both high and low. He was admired and loved by the humble and hated by the great. He was 'a priest of

Seinte Marie, in York' but had no fixed job or home. For twenty years he had tramped about England preaching, living on the charity of those who heard him. Wherever he found a few people ready to listen, by the roadside, on a village green or in a market place, he would pour forth fiery words against the evils of the day and particularly the sins of the rich. He raged against greed and pride in high places to people who were poor and low. He condemned the sins of lords to those who had suffered at their hands. 'In the beginning of the world', he would cry 'there were no villeins and ought not to be now. Men should not be kept in *bondage* like beasts.' It was no wonder that the poor and the discontented listened to him as if spell-bound, and not surprising that he had been three times clapped into prison as a dangerous trouble-maker. The last time had been for three months in Canterbury gaol because he insisted on preaching in the cathedral cloisters just when people were coming away from the mass.

Now John Ball had been set free and was safe among the commons of Kent, and he was bursting to pour out the passionate words which had been bottled up for three months, words which were exactly what his audience wanted to hear. Whenever there was a chance he launched into a sermon. 'O ye good people,' began one of them, 'matters goeth not well in England, nor shall not till everything be common, and there be no villeins nor gentlemen, ... and lords be no greater than we. Let us go to the King, he is young, and show him what

The King's mother would travel in a covered carriage like this, with her ladies-in-waiting and her pet dogs – if she had any

bondage we be in...and when the King seeth us we shall have remedy.' Such words put fresh heart into the marchers, however short their food was running, however sharply the stones cut into their worn shoes, and they must have repeated the juiciest bits to each other, and perhaps used as a marching song the catchy rhyme from another of his sermons.

> When Adam dug and Eve span,
> Who was then the gentleman.

John Ball made up many mysterious messages which seemed to pass swiftly about the country among the rebels, and encouraged them or warned them. They were easily remembered and were in a kind of code, and though they may puzzle us when we read them now, they were quite clear to the people who got them in 1381. They knew perfectly well what was meant by: 'Jon Balle gretyth you wel and doth yew to understand that he hath rungen youre bel. Now ryhte and myght, wyll and skyll. God spede everie manne. Nowe is the tyme.'

Another letter was sent to the commons of Essex urging them to finish what they had begun. It was later found in the jerkin of a man who was to be hanged. It said 'Jon Schepe, som tyme Seynte Marie prest of York...greteth Jon Nameles, and Jon the miller, and Jon Cartere and biddeth them that they bee ware of *gyle*, and stande together in God's name. And biddeth Piers Plowman go to his werk and chastise Hobbe the robbere.' This really does need explaining. 'Jon Schepe' was a nickname for himself; the others are not actual people but meant all sorts of workers who were to stand together, do their work if they were still at home, and punish the dishonest people who disgraced the cause of the commons.

At last, urged on by Wat Tyler and inspired by John Ball, 'the commons of Kent to the number of 50,000' arrived near the south bank of the Thames. It was the evening of Wednesday

Opposite: *John Ball preaching. Probably the artist who painted this was not an eye-witness but used his imagination. We never hear of John Ball preaching on horseback. And look at his followers, would they have been so well armed and would they have stood in such neat ranks?*

13 June. Across the river could be seen the walls of London, the houses packed close inside them, and the Tower where the young King was. It seemed they had only to go over the bridge and through the gates to reach him, but the drawbridge was up and the gates shut fast. That night most of the rebels camped on Blackheath and slept as well as empty stomachs and sore feet would allow. One chronicler says that a quarter of them 'fasted for lack of *victuals*, for they had none, wherewith they were sore displeased', and with good reason. But some who still had the energy left, found their way into the dark little streets of Southwark nearer still to the bridge. There they met up with certain men from London and from Essex who had slipped across the river to greet them. In the short summer night they broke open another prison, the Marshalsea, and set free the prisoners, and pushing on another 3 kilometres burnt the palace of the Archbishop at Lambeth, and the house of the prison governor. No doubt they stole food and drink from both places and then dropped asleep in the streets while the flames lit up the sky.

Those flames were watched with fear and dismay by many Londoners, and by the King and his Council from the Tower, who knew that besides the thousands of men on the south bank there were also thousands to the east of the city. These were the commons of Essex, close to the walls. London was besieged.

4 Londoners Open the Gates

London is now a huge city spreading for miles along both banks of the Thames and more than 7 million people live there. It is very difficult to imagine how small it was in 1381 with a population of only 35 thousand. Even with that small number it was the largest town in England. It was surrounded by walls pierced by seven main gates (see map on page 40), each of them big enough to let horses and carts pass through, and these were shut and barred at night, from sunset to sunrise. There were a few secret and unguarded entrances, especially down by the river. Only one bridge, London Bridge, carried traffic over the Thames, but it was quite easy at any hour to slip across by water in a small boat from one of the many little boat-houses and *wharves* along the river bank.

Most of London's buildings, the houses, shops, churches, markets and warehouses were packed closely together inside the walls, but they had begun to spread beyond, for the city was growing. In the open country you would find the hospital of St Bartholomew (now famous all over the world), a number of churches and monastic houses, the beautiful new palace of the Savoy, just built by John of Gaunt, the royal palace of Westminster and the great church itself built by Edward the Confessor. The map on page 40 shows some of these places.

In the city the streets were narrow, dirty, and smelly, some paved with *cobbles*, some just dirt tracks. Many of the houses were tall and narrow, with high pointed roofs, and often the upper floors hung over the streets so far that in some of the narrowest you could easily shake hands with your opposite neighbour from the upstairs windows. The streets were seldom

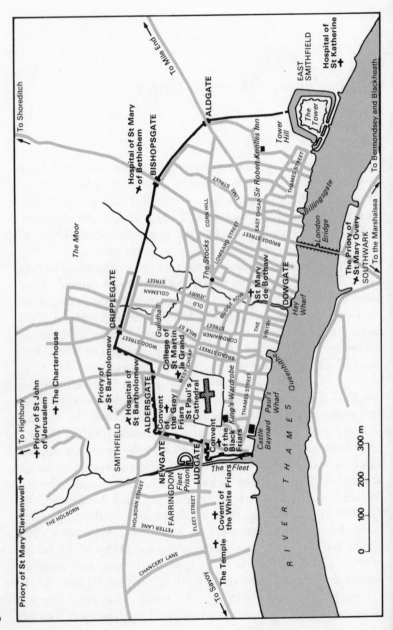

straight; there were filthy little hovels, where poor folk lived, tucked in among the grander houses, and all sorts of dark corners and passages where ruffians could hide, ready to jump out on a harmless passer-by. Quiet folk kept out of the streets as much as possible, especially at night, and especially if they were foreigners, whose lives and purses were always in peril.

Thieves were a constant danger. Two other dangers were fire and plague. The houses were mainly built of wood, often with thatched roofs, and if a fire once started it could spread with terrible speed, the sparks leaping from house to house. Plague and other diseases were always present because there were no proper drains and no clean water supply.

People usually threw their rubbish into the streets to rot and stink, to feed rats and breed flies. The noses of Londoners were much less sensitive to bad smells than they are now, and they knew very little about hygiene. The Mayor and Council were always trying to stop the dumping of rubbish in the streets and in the river. 'No one shall throw into the Thames any rushes, straw, rubbish or filth' they ordered, but nothing stopped it, even though the river was used for drinking water. It was also used for washing, and you could often see people filling their jugs and leather buckets with water to drink in one place, while a few yards upstream women were busy scrubbing dirty clothes. If you got your water near Billingsgate, the smell when fish were being unloaded was terrible. Fish caused a lot of trouble because they so often went bad. The punishment for trying to sell bad fish was to stand for at least one hour in the pillory and have the fish burnt under your nose, so you can be sure that a great many rotten conger eels and herrings were tossed overboard into the Thames to add to the stink!

In these ways, with its dirt, its smells, its dangers, London was like other medieval towns, but in certain other ways it was different. It was specially important because it was the

Opposite: *This map of London shows the walls, gates and all the places mentioned in the chapter. The inn called Sir Robert Knolles Inn was named after the old knight who led the citizens of London to Smithfield when William Walworth called on them to come to the help of the King*

capital of the kingdom. The King with his court was often to be seen in the streets, and he lived a good deal in one of his houses in the city, or just outside at the palace of Westminster. At Westminster, too, Parliament often met. Royal orders and *proclamations* went out from London and the chief law courts were there. It was the centre of government.

Besides being the capital and the largest town in England, London was also the busiest. Much of its trade came by water, and the Thames was like a busy highway, along which ships of every size and shape passed. Small rowing boats bobbed across from one bank to the other, and much bigger sea-going ships sailed up and down. These came from every port round English coasts, as well as from foreign lands. They tied up along the wharves, or lay at anchor in the river, emptied out one cargo and took another on board. From English ports came fish, corn, vegetables, wool, sheep skins and timber. From foreign lands came furs and spices, silks, wine and fruit like dates and raisins. This foreign trade meant that foreign merchants and sea-captains were always to be seen in the streets. Some only came and went with their ships but some had to live in the city to do business and often they had a hard time of it. There were Germans, Lombards from Italy, and Flemings from Flanders (where Holland and Belgium now are) and they probably disliked the Londoners as much as they were disliked themselves. London mobs thought that all foreigners traded unfairly and took jobs away from Englishmen.

In the first days of June 1381 the city of London was an uneasy place, hot and stuffy and restless. Scraps of news flew about in streets and shops, news of villagers breaking the laws, refusing to pay taxes and beating up royal officers. Then came rumours of great bands of the same law-breakers marching towards London. The exact numbers cannot be known, for the reports vary from 10,000 to 60,000 and more, but it is safe to say that there were many thousands. Now these rebels were at the very gates of London to the south and the east. What was going to happen? Why had nothing been done to stop them when the rioting and law-breaking first began, or on the way from Canterbury? Why hadn't William Walworth, the Mayor, called out armed bands of citizens to protect the lives and property of Londoners? After all, this had been done in 1377 to protect the ships in the Thames from French pirates. Why didn't the King and his Council collect an army and scatter the rebels? You can imagine how the bewildered people of London must have asked these puzzling questions again and again and found no answer. We find them puzzling too, but looking back from a distance of nearly 600 years we can discover at least some of the answers.

First of all, we know that such a great revolt as this was something quite new in England. Today we may be getting used to protests, marches, and violent clashes but people in 1381 were not. Villagers might have short sharp quarrels with their lords, and unjust stewards like John le Doo. Wild apprentices and workmen might sometimes be unruly in the streets. But these were small matters compared with a rising of thousands. The Peasants' Revolt was 'a great and unexpected *calamity*' by which, so Froissart thought, 'England was at a point to be lost'. Nearly everyone was taken by surprise; perhaps even the rebels themselves were.

The King was still only fourteen, and had very little to do with the government of the country. That was in the hands of his ministers and his uncles. If tough grown men did not know what to do, how could a lad of fourteen? At least he showed no lack of courage. His three soldier uncles were all away – John of Gaunt in Scotland, Thomas of Woodstock in Wales and Edmund of Cambridge in Portugal – so there were no military men to advise him. In any case they were so unpopular, especially John of Gaunt, that they would have been little help in London.

William Walworth, Mayor of London, and most of his aldermen were loyal and steady and could guess what would happen if thousands of reckless, hungry (and thirsty) men got into London. They would certainly get drunk and do much damage by burning and looting. More than this, everyone – the King, his ministers, the Mayor and aldermen – all knew

43

Town workers. They seem to be having an argument. These are the 'commons of London' who welcomed the rebels into the city and led them to the Temple and the Savoy palace

that there was grave danger inside the walls as well as outside. It came from the commons of London who were just as discontented and restless as the commons of the country. They, too, hated the poll tax and all those who collected it, or who punished poor men who did not pay: the royal officials and the lawyers and judges. They, too, suffered from the Statutes of Labourers and the freeze on wages. They hated the rich and powerful, the ministers and the wealthy merchants and master-craftsmen of London.

There were hundreds of *journeymen* who found it impossible to rise to the position of master-craftsmen. The wealthy and important members of the guilds had practically closed them to all but the rich by making it very expensive to belong, to pay the entrance fees and all the other expenses. It had become the custom for master-craftsmen to wear livery, a sort of uniform, on special occasions, and this was expensive. So were the guild feasts. Roast pig, goose, lamb and venison, and best hen baked in pastry were not cheap. Nor were salmon, oysters, and 'exquisite herrings'. On top of that were red and white and sweet wines to say nothing about 'afters' of 'dates, figges, raysons greate and smalle, pears, cheryes, and ginger-flavoured pastries'. Such feasts were much too costly for a humble craftsman, however skilful he might be. *Apprentices* also soon discovered that at the end of their training they had little to look forward to except grinding poverty and fear of un-employment. Many such townsmen were as resentful as any villein bound to a harsh lord. In London this resentment was at boiling point and the commons were only waiting for the right moment to show it and to show their power. Now perhaps that moment had come, and no one in authority dared do anything to provoke the mobs to come out into the streets.

So in the days between 30 May and 13 June the feeling in London must have been very tense, as if some great thunder-storm was mounting up, an atmosphere full of dread and dismay for some, full of hidden excitement and secret plans for others.

Outside the walls, the rebels were in good spirits. At Black-heath early on 13 June John Ball preached one of his most fiery sermons, for which he would certainly have been clapped into prison if he had been caught. 'Take good courage', he shouted, 'and make away with them all, kill the great lords of the kingdom, slay all judges, lawyers, root out every man that is harmful to the common good, for when the great ones have been cut off all men will be free.' These were dangerous words, an open encouragement to murder.

Almost as he spoke, a message came to say that the King was coming to meet the men of Kent and would arrive by boat on the shore below Blackheath. Soon the watching crowd on the river bank saw the royal barge leave the Tower and drop down the river towards them. You can imagine their excitement and triumph. The King was coming! They would meet him face to face, they would warn him about his evil ministers, tell him their grievances and make their demands. Ten thousand people in such a state could not keep calm and quiet and the crowd burst out into 'such a cry as if the devil in hell had been among them'. The shouts and yells must have been deafening, some cheering for the King, others howling for the heads of the Archbishop, the Treasurer and John of Gaunt. As the barge drew nearer to the shore the excitement and the

Richard II at Greenwich. Again the artist was probably not an eye-witness. The rebels must have looked far more wild and desperate, as we know they shouted as if 'the devil in hell' was among them

noise grew wilder and more frantic until it was plain that the King could not possibly land. He would have been trampled underfoot by the crowds, however loyal to him they might be. So the barge was stopped a few yards out from the bank and Richard tried to make himself heard. 'Sirs', he shouted, 'What do you want? Tell me this, now that I have come.' Then the crowd roared back: 'We would that you should come *aland*, and then we shall show you what we lack.'

It was a hopeless position and those around the King said to him, 'it was too great folly to go there, for they were men without reason and had not the sense to behave properly'.

A peasant drawing his bow

They advised him not to land and so the royal barge began to pull away from the shore. It was a moment of great danger for there were enough bows and arrows among the commons to pierce every person on the barge. But shouts of anger and disappointment were the only things that followed the King as the oarsmen strained to get out of reach. 'And when the people saw how the King was returned to the Tower they were inflamed with anger. Then they cried all with one voice "Let us go to London" and so they took their way thither', to London bridge. They were determined to get into the city and very soon they did.

There are two explanations of the way the rebels got in. One is that five treacherous *aldermen* of the city helped them. These men were enemies of the Mayor and wanted to disgrace him and get power for themselves on the council. He had already ordered that all the gates of London were to be closed and the drawbridge raised. He also sent certain aldermen to the gates to see that his orders were obeyed and that there were enough guards, and to deliver a message to the rebels outside telling them to come no nearer the city but to go home. The five aldermen were among the ones given this duty to carry out, but they did not do it. On the night of 12 June one of them opened the Aldgate on the east side of the city (see the map on page 40) and allowed the men of Essex to enter. That same night another one, John Horne, had a secret meeting with several Kentish rebels, perhaps with Wat Tyler himself, and took some of them back to his own house for the night. Next morning he went to one of the city officers and said, 'The Mayor has commanded you to lend me a *standard* bearing the royal arms.' After much argument the officer unwillingly handed over the standard, and Horne, who must have been able to use a private gate and a boat, left the city, crossed the river, and rode towards Blackheath. He is supposed to have met the rebels streaming down towards London bridge, and with the royal standard above him, said, 'Come to London because all of us therein are your friends, and ready to do what you will. We offer you our favour and help in all you do.' He then used his authority as an alderman to have the drawbridge lowered and the gate opened and the rebels of Kent poured into London.

If this is true, it was an act of black treachery not only to the Mayor but to the King as well. When the revolt was finally over John Horne and the others were brought before the sheriffs of London and accused of conspiring 'treacherously and deceitfully with the chief leaders of the rebels and of treacherously bringing Walter Tyler and many other leaders with their bands of innumerable fellows into the city'. They were found guilty and put in prison, and if the story is true they deserved this punishment. But the odd thing is that less than two years later they were tried again, found not guilty and set free. Possibly the story is not true but was invented by their enemies!

The other explanation, which Froissart gives, is much simpler. He says that the poor commons of London 'drew together and said among themselves, "Why do we not let these good people enter the city? They are our fellows, and what they do is for us." Then they went to the bridge and cried to the keepers to let them in or they [the keepers] would be *undone*.' At this threat and in fear of their lives the keepers lowered the drawbridge and let the marchers enter, though it was greatly against their will. The commons of London did the same at other gates so that the men of Essex and of Kent were able to get into the city without trouble. Once inside they met no resistance.

The first thing most of them wanted was food and drink. Some of them had been on the move for over a week and had long ago finished the scanty food they had brought from home, the crumbs of coarse bread and bits of fat bacon, or the scraps they had somehow managed to collect on the way. Now they went, asked or unasked, into the nearest houses and sat down to eat and drink. One chronicle says that 'everything they asked for was brought, for everyone was ready to give them meat and drink to *appease* them'. In other words, people were afraid and it is not surprising. It would have needed a very brave man or woman to refuse food to a dozen rough countrymen armed with sticks and knives. You can imagine how eagerly the marchers fell on the meal they were given, and stuffed themselves with London food, some of it far finer than any they had ever eaten. When they were full and could eat no more, they went out into the streets.

5 Mob Violence

The rebels entered London on the morning of 13 June. At first they behaved quietly. They had satisfied their hunger, and, as most of them had never been to London before, you can imagine that they were amazed beyond words at the sight of so many buildings and people. But this mood did not last long. For one thing they joined up with London commons who were on their home ground and intent on ill-doing. For another, many citizens rashly left their wine cellars open 'to appease' them. As the day became hotter and the commons drank more and more, they became, not just tipsy as they might at home after a mug or two of ale, but roaring drunk and dangerous. Together with the commons of London the rebels from Kent and Essex began to run riot through the streets leaving a trail of destruction behind them. They found the noise of falling timber and the sound of crackling fires very pleasant and exciting.

The London mob were determined to attack the palace of John of Gaunt, the King's uncle, a *bogey*-man to the poor, and one of the most hated people in England. Savoy palace lay outside the walls to the west of London. It was newly built and full of treasures, some of them looted from the French wars. In the afternoon of 13 June a mixed mob of commons from London, Essex and Kent rampaged through the streets towards the Ludgate which was in the western wall (see map on page 40). On the way they burnt down some houses and shops, broke open the Fleet prison and freed all the prisoners. Then they went to the Temple, headquarters of the lawyers, those men who, after the King's ministers, were most detested

These shops are closely packed together and you can imagine how quickly fire would spread through the streets, especially as there was much timber in the buildings

by the commons, for they said, 'It was their cursed parchments which were the ruin of honest men.'

The Temple was the place where students were trained to be lawyers, and where they had their library and store of documents. By now all the lawyers and students had fled, and the commons found the place empty, but they set to work to 'cast down' the buildings, which is a way of saying they pulled them down and destroyed them. We hear of protesters today who pull up paving stones, tear down railings and throw the slates down from roofs. Angry people can be very strong. But we don't hear that they actually pull down houses with their bare hands. However in the Middle Ages many buildings were much flimsier than ours are, and being made of *wattle and daub*, they really could be torn apart and 'cast down'. At the Temple the rebels climbed on the roofs, threw off the tiles and thatch, cast down walls, and burnt all the books and parchments on the street outside. During the next two days they did the same over and over again to houses, shops, churches and prisons.

Next the crowd of rebels left London by the Ludgate and made for John of Gaunt's palace. They broke in without difficulty. As usual the guards either fled or gave way in terror. Once inside the mob destroyed everything. They hacked the furniture to bits, smashed the windows, burnt the silken tapestries, the beds and their coverlets, they pounded into shapeless lumps the silver and gold cups and plates, even the fine armour, and they ground jewels to powder under their feet. Then with torches they set fire to the whole place. As the palace burnt three barrels were found, and these they cheerfully tossed into the flames not knowing what was in them. It was gunpowder, and after that the fire must have burnt very fiercely indeed. Some rebels died in the explosion and others, who had discovered the wine cellar, drank so much that they did not notice when their way out was blocked by burning wood and fallen walls. In the noise of the fire and wild shouting no one heard their cries and they were burnt to death.

Another band of rebels, still outside the walls on the west of the city, attacked the Priory of St John (see map) because it was used by the Treasurer, the 'traitor' Sir John Hales. It was also the home of the ancient and noble order of the Knights Hospitallers, who spent their lives caring for pilgrims, especially those in the Holy Land. The priory, the church, and the hospital itself were given the usual treatment and burnt to the ground. It was another example of senseless destruction 'a great and horrible piece of damage to the priory for all time to come'. Seven wretched foreigners were found in the church,

*The Tower of London. Richard watched the fires lit by the rebels from 'a high garret'
in this building*

probably silk-weavers from Holland. They were dragged out
and killed. Some of those present must have hesitated before
doing this to men who had taken refuge in a church, but the
London mob had a blind hatred of foreign workers and
stopped at nothing.

So the day went on with clamour in the streets, prisons
opened, houses cast down and burnt, people beaten up. One
chronicler says that eighteen were killed. And all the time a
great crowd of commons surrounded the Tower, seeking the
King, who remained 'anxiously and sadly' inside, seeing the
fires break out and hearing the shouts below and around the
fortress. He could do nothing but send out messages and
proclamations. One of these urged the rebels to leave London
and go home. If they did, then he would 'grant them pardon

53

William Walworth, Mayor of London in 1381

for all manner of *trespasses* and *felonies* done up to this hour'. Two of his knights carried the message out and one of them, standing on an old chair, read it in a loud voice to the crowd. It was badly received and a great cry rose that it was 'nothing but a trifle and a mockery'. Yesterday the King had said he would speak with the people, and he had broken his word. Now they would show him their strength and their demands. They burnt more houses and sent in to the King a list of the 'traitors' round him whom they meant to kill: Archbishop Sudbury, Sir Robert Hales, and fifteen others, some of whom were in the Tower with the King.

Towards the end of the day Richard climbed to 'a high garret' to watch the flames, now leaping up in scores of places. He must have realised that he was besieged. When he came down he again sent for his lords and council and again asked what they advised him to do. 'They did not know how to advise him and were *abashed*', and you can well imagine them scratching their heads and shuffling their feet. Not only were they abashed, they were also divided. Some of them, including William Walworth, who was no coward, wanted to sally out from the Tower when it was dark and attack the rebels as they slept. There were 600 armed men and 600 archers in the Tower and Walworth could also have called on many steady citizens to arm themselves and help. These advisers guessed that the commons would be so drunk that they could be 'slain like flies'; they also knew that only one in twenty was properly armed. However, another group said it would be wiser to appease the crowd and give them all they asked, for if force should fail there was nothing left to try. The appeasers won the argument and no action was taken.

But it must have been clear to all of them that they were in a trap. No one could get out of the Tower unless the crowds outside would allow it, and no one could get in. Even food supplies were threatened, for one group of rebels were insolent enough to stop the King's food from being carried in. It was then suggested by someone on the council that the King might again agree to meet the rebels, talk with them and try to calm them down and get them to go home.

Richard, who had much more spirit than most of his advisers, quickly agreed and yet another proclamation was sent out saying that all were to go to Mile End early next day and the King would ride out to meet them. Mile End was in the fields to the east of the city, a place much loved by Londoners and one where they went in summer to enjoy the fresh air. The idea was to draw the crowds out of the streets and away from the Tower into the peaceful country. Then their fury might die down and they could be persuaded to go home. Also, if they went away from the Tower the ministers inside, whose lives were in such deadly peril, might manage to escape.

Very early on the morning of 14 June Richard rode out of the Tower. He was attended by the earls of Buckingham, Kent, Oxford and Warwick, by the Mayor and aldermen and by many knights and squires. The great sword of state was carried before him. He left behind him in the Tower his mother and her women and body-guard, and of course the Archbishop and the Treasurer, who would have instantly been set upon if they had dared to show their faces to the commons.

It was a dangerous journey for the young King, for even with his escort he could have been overwhelmed and killed by the huge crowd, some of them lurking in the streets, some marching alongside the royal party towards Mile End. One chronicle says that he 'went in great dread of his life', and it is not surprising. Only two of the King's men lost their nerve as they rode along among the noisy mob. They were the Earl of Kent and Sir John Holland who, at a place where the crowd was less thick, edged their horses through it and galloped away into the countryside. They were the King's half-brothers. No one else deserted him.

The King reached Mile End at seven o'clock. When he arrived and the crowd saw him among them they forgot their anger and disappointment of the day before when he had not landed at Blackheath, and only remembered that he was their King. They knelt down before him, saying 'Welcome, our Lord King Richard, if it pleases you, we will not have any other king but you.' Then the King spoke sweetly to them. He had come ready to promise almost anything in order 'to settle their fury' and disperse them and they must have been surprised when he agreed to their demands one after another. Wat Tyler was their spokesman and they demanded five things.

1. Serfdom should be abolished.
2. All forced service and dues should disappear.

3. All holders of land should be free tenants and pay a rent of only two pence an acre to the landlord.
4. A general pardon should be granted to all who had taken part in the rising.
5. The commons should seize and deal with all the traitors who had sinned against the king and the law.

Richard granted the first four but to the fifth which was really a demand to be allowed to hunt down and kill anyone against whom they bore a grudge, he answered carefully. They might seize traitors but must then bring them before him and he would deal with them according to the law of the land. Then he said, 'Withdraw you home to your houses and into such villages as ye came from, and leave behind of every village two or three, and I shall cause writings to be made and seal them with my seal and they shall have them.'

These words pleased many of the commons, particularly 'such as were simple and good plain men', and especially the men of Essex. They received the King's promise willingly saying 'It is well said and we desire no more'. They chose the men who were to stay and wait for the written *charters*, and then trusting the word of the King, set off back to their villages for they were 'weary with their long labours and longed to see their homes, wives and children once again'.

But, just as at Rochester, there were some who were not yet satisfied and did not go home. These were Londoners and the men of Kent who remained behind and showed themselves 'persistent in their evil actions... and continued to kill men and to burn and cast down houses' for the rest of that day and part of the next.

While all this was going on, terrible things were happening at the Tower of London. Wat Tyler was always a suspicious person, and he was far too cunning not to guess at one of the reasons for the King riding out to Mile End. He did not leave the Tower unguarded but left behind a small body of chosen men to watch the gates. When Archbishop Sudbury tried to slip out by boat from the little water-gate on the Thames he was seen and forced to go back, so that all the so-called traitors were still penned up in the Tower. As soon as the meeting with the King was over, Wat Tyler and another group of chosen men, who had been told what to do, left Mile End and hurried back to the city. They meant to do as the King had said 'seize and arrest all traitors' but they certainly did not intend to bring them to him for a proper trial!

Soon hundreds of these determined men were at the main gate of the Tower, demanding to be let in. Now, according to Thomas Walsingham, the Tower was strongly guarded by '600 soldiers, strong and most expert, as well as 600 archers' and it is one of the mysteries of the revolt that they made no attempt whatever to keep the rebels out. Instead, says Walsingham, 'They all, marvellously enough, appeared more like the dead than the living'! They seem to have had just enough life in them to open the gate and so the rebels easily entered the Tower, yet another victory for them. They surged along the passages and up and down the stone stairs, some hunting for those they meant to kill, others simply curious and ready to enjoy themselves in a rough way. They joked with the soldiers standing helplessly by and urged them to join in the search for traitors. They jeered at knights and squires and with their dirty hands stroked their fine clothes, their faces and beards. They broke into room after room until they reached the royal apartments.

Walsingham writes with horror of what happened next. 'Who would believe that such rustics, and most inferior ones at that, would dare to enter the chamber of the King and of his mother with their filthy sticks?' In Richard's room they looked for traitors under the bed, and then sat and rolled on it, laughing at his attendants. Next they went to the chamber of the Princess of Wales. The poor woman had hardly recovered from the shock of meeting the commons of Kent on the Canterbury road and was probably resting. This second meeting was far worse, for 'these gluttons, rushing in, brake her bed, whereby she was so sore *affrayed* that she swooned', which, considering the noise, the sight of sweaty faces and filthy sticks and the fact that one ruffian is said to have kissed her, is not very surprising. But at least she escaped without injury. Most of the commons were still loyal to the King and would not harm his mother. Besides they were after more important victims, the Chancellor, the Treasurer, and any others from their black list that they could find.

After his attempt to escape in the early morning had failed Archbishop Sudbury knew in his heart that he was doomed. However inefficient he may have been as Chancellor – he was not a very clever man – in this last terrible crisis he shows up as a brave and saintly person. He spent all Thursday night in prayer and now, having heard the Mass in the chapel, was still there on his knees. He must have heard the noise and shouting coming nearer and nearer and when the rebels burst in yelling 'Where is that traitor and spoiler of the people?', he stood up and faced them calmly. 'Good my sons,' he said 'you have come, behold I am the Archbishop whom ye seek, but not a traitor, or a spoiler.' Thomas Walsingham, monk as he was, must have nearly choked with horror as he wrote his vivid description of what then happened.

> 'On seeing him, those limbs of Satan laid their unpious [wicked] hands on him and tore him from the chapel, paying no respect to the holiness of the place, or its holy altars, nor to the Cross at the top of his *crozier*, nor even to the sacrament which a priest held before him. They disregarded the presence of God and dragged the Archbishop along the passages by his arms and his hood to their fellows outside the gates on Tower Hill.'

There they beheaded him, so clumsily that it took eight strokes of a sword to do it. They also killed Sir Robert Hales, the Treasurer of England, and Brother William Appleton, a monk and a skilled doctor. The heads were mounted on poles and carried before the triumphant crowd through the streets till at last they stuck them up on the gate of London Bridge. The Archbishop's head was marked out by a red *mitre* fixed to it by a nail.

The murder of Archbishop Sudbury, together with Sir Robert Hales, Treasurer of England (kneeling) and Brother Appleton, a monk and famous doctor

The rest of that long day and the next night must have been the most horrible hours of the whole rising. The mob was in a mad and cruel mood and raged through the streets looking for more victims 'with hideous cries and tumult'. They may have killed as many as 160 people, most of them either lawyers or foreigners. It is said that anyone thought to be foreign was seized and told to say 'bread and cheese'. If he spoke with an accent and said 'brod and case' he was instantly killed. In spite of Richard's visit to Mile End and his sweet words the commons were not yet appeased.

6 Richard Rides Out

The King did not go back to the Tower on Friday. Instead he rode through the City to a small royal house called the Wardrobe, not far from the Ludgate. He found his mother there in a state of great distress. After the crowds had left the Tower to gloat over the murder of the 'traitors', her servants had carried her out to a boat lying close under the wall. They covered her up so that none could see her and rowed her up the river to the Wardrobe, where she usually stayed when she was in London. There she lay for the rest of Friday 'like a woman half-dead, till she was comforted by her son, the King'.

Richard had many other things on his mind besides the comfort of his mother. He had promised charters to the Essex men at Mile End and the royal clerks had to do these as soon as possible. They were kept busy for many hours writing them. Each charter was addressed to the royal officials in the various parts of Essex, and each one began:

> Richard, by the grace of God, King of England and France, and Lord of Ireland, to all his bailiffs and all faithful men to whom these letters come, Greetings.

Then the King's promises were set out and the charter ended by saying:

> We also pardon our said subjects from all felonies, acts of treason, transgressions and extortions, done by them. Witnessed by myself at London on 15 June in the fourth year of my reign.

62　The next thing to decide was more difficult. What was to be done now? The Wardrobe was unfortified, and the King was not safe there. If Wat Tyler had ordered the gangs, roaming through London, to attack it, they could easily make him a prisoner, if nothing worse. They were still burning and looting and terrifying the law-abiding citizens. Many of them were so drunk that they lay in the streets 'like slaughtered pigs' sleeping off the effects of too much stolen wine and ale. Richard must have wondered whether his visit to Mile End had done any good at all. His council again chewed over the problems, but still made no attempt to use force against the rebels. Instead they proposed that another attempt must be made to appease them and that the King should meet them again on an open space called Smithfield (the smooth field) outside Aldersgate. Richard agreed and a proclamation was read in four different parts of London, bidding the commons meet him at Smithfield in the afternoon of Saturday, 15 June.

He must have known that this meeting would be far more dangerous than the one at Mile End. The 'simple, and good plain men' had gone home. The violent and dangerous ones remained, and they were now much more certain of their power. After all, they had stormed the Tower, seen royal soldiers stand aside for them, and killed the chief 'traitors' on their black list. They had let hell loose in London streets without a sword being drawn, or an arrow shot against them. They were ready to do anything for their captain Wat Tyler and power had already gone to his head. He boasted frequently that in a few days there would be no laws in England but those that came out of his mouth. However he agreed to meet the King at Smithfield, and ordered the commons to do the same, but no one knows what he planned to do there. He certainly did not mean the revolt to end. He may have hoped to seize the King and hold him as a hostage till all the demands of the rebels were granted and all their enemies killed.

Richard rode out from the Wardrobe early on Saturday, attended by about 200 nobles, knights, and squires, by William Walworth the Mayor, and the loyal aldermen. He went to Westminster Abbey where he confessed his sins and said his 63 prayers and then set off for Smithfield. If you look at a map of London today it is hard to believe that he rode through green fields 'where the babbling of brooks and the clack of mills' were to be heard. When he got to Smithfield he sat on his horse with his back to St Bartholomew's hospital and waited, facing a huge crowd of commons standing in lines 'of great size'. There were thousands of them and against them the royal party of 200 must have looked very small and weak. It was about two o'clock, on a hot summer afternoon.

There are several very different accounts in the chronicles of what happened in the next hour or so. They all agree on some things, such as the insolence and bad temper of Wat Tyler, and the King's efforts to appease the commons. All of them are against the commons and their captain, but we must try to imagine what it was like for Wat Tyler. In about a week he had changed from being a quite unknown person, a soldier perhaps, or a mender of roofs, to being the leader of a huge army of men ready to obey his orders. He had led them to the heart of the kingdom, and twice had forced the King of England to come and speak with him. He had brought about the deaths of two great ministers and had put all London in terror. He must have had a feeling of triumph and power, as if he had only to ask – or demand – and he would get exactly what he wanted. In this mood he, too, waited, sitting on a small horse so that his followers could see him.

Then the King sent word across to him by the Mayor that he should approach and speak with him and he rode forward. When he came near to the King Wat Tyler got off his horse, but instead of dropping on his knees and taking off his hat, as the custom was when speaking to the King, he half bent one knee and then shook the King's hand 'roughly and forcefully'.

'Brother,' he said rudely, 'be of good cheer, for in the fortnight that is to come, you shall have 40,000 more commons, and we shall be good companions.'

Then he stood, tossing a dagger to and fro in his hands 'like a boy playing a game' but it was a threatening game, for he was near enough to Richard to stab him. The men round

64

the King must have been speechless with rage at the man's insolence but they dared not move or protest for fear of the crowd opposite and because of the dagger so near their master.

Then the King said, 'Why will you not go back to your own country?' and Wat answered with a great oath that they would not go until they had their charter as they wished to have it, and he added that the lords of England would regret it bitterly if the will of the commons was not done. He repeated the demands made at Mile End but added several more:

1. No man should be outlawed.
2. No lord should have any lordship, except the King.
3. The wealth and lands of the church should be taken away and divided among the people.
4. There should be only one bishop (no doubt this one was to be John Ball).
5. The commons should be free to fish or hunt in all water, fish-ponds, woods and forests.

Richard replied quietly that the commons should have all that they asked which he, the King, could grant by the law of the land. Then he ordered Wat to return to his own home. It was a vague answer but the King had no power to agree at once to all these demands. He could not suddenly get rid of all bishops, hand out the wealth of the church, or take away all the lord-ships (property) of the nobles. Wat Tyler probably realised that he was not getting what he wanted. He lost his temper. He called loudly for a jug of water 'because of the great heat he felt' and when it came 'he rinsed out his mouth in a very rude and villainous way' which probably means that he spat the water out at the King's feet! Next he called for a jug of ale and 'drank a great draught'. After this insolence he climbed on to his horse.

At this tense moment a voice from among the King's men was heard saying, 'This man is the greatest robber and thief in Kent.' The voice came from a squire, who lived in Kent himself and who had been staring hard at the rebel leader. Wat Tyler, of course, heard, and in fury turned to strike the speaker with his dagger. He would have killed him in the King's presence, which was a serious crime, if William Walworth the Mayor of London had not reproved him for his behaviour and contempt of the King, and pushed forward to arrest him. At once Wat stabbed the Mayor in the stomach in great fury. The Mayor, wise man that he was, was wearing armour under his coat and was unhurt. He drew his own dagger and struck back giving Wat Tyler a great cut in the neck and another on the head. There was a general scuffle in which another of the King's men drew his sword and 'ran the rebel leader two or three times through the body, mortally wounding him'. Wat managed to spur his horse and ride about ninety metres towards the commons, but he then fell to the ground half-dead. A great cry went up from the commons when they saw him fall. 'Our captain is dead...slain by treachery. Let us avenge his death.' They pulled out their arrows, bent their bows and got ready to shoot.

It was a moment of extreme danger for the King and his men. If the hail of arrows had been loosed they would have been killed. But it was also a moment of marvellous courage on the part of Richard. In an instant he spurred his horse, cantered out towards the furious crowd, and rode among them crying, 'Sirs, will you shoot your King? I will be your chief and your captain, and you shall have from me all that you seek, only follow me into the fields without.' He pointed to the open fields near the burnt-out remains of St John's priory, and then rode very slowly towards them. After a moment's hesitation the crowd began to stream after him in a bewildered way, uncertain whether to kill him, or to get the royal charters and hurry off home. Some of the King's household followed their master, half-hidden among the commons, others were so frightened that they left him to the mercy of the crowd and disappeared. The sturdy William Walworth, at last free to do

Opposite: *Smithfield. The artist here has combined two pictures in one. On the left William Walworth is striking Wat Tyler. On the right the King is riding towards the rebels saying 'I am your King, I will be your leader'*

what he had longed to do, galloped into London and began
to shout, 'Most noble, gracious, and pious citizens, arm your-
selves and go to help your King without delay for he is threatened with death.'

It was the sort of appeal which ought to have been made
long before and there must have been many who were ready
and waiting for something to do. One chronicle said: 'When
they heard this, the notable men of London, and others who
loved the King immediately armed themselves to the number
of 1000 men.' They went out into the streets ready to be led
to Smithfield, and a stout-hearted old knight, Sir John Knolles,
at once put himself at their head. By the time the King had
drawn the commons away from the houses and into the open
fields, 'a fine company of well-armed men in great strength'
arrived, followed by the Mayor with a 'good company carrying
lances'. He searched for Wat Tyler and was told he had been
carried into St Bartholomew's hospital. The Mayor, now
completely ruthless, had the dying man carried out and beheaded. His head was set on a pole and carried to the King
who was still among the commons. When the rebels saw that
their captain was indeed dead, all the heart went out of them.
'They threw down their rough weapons, sticks and axes, bows
and arrows and fell upon the ground, there among the corn
like beaten men and implored the King for mercy. And the
King granted them mercy.'

By now the commons were completely surrounded 'like
sheep in a pen' by the fine company of well-armed men and
Richard commanded two of his knights to lead them back
through London and over the bridge and so see them peacefully on their way home without doing them any harm. Some
of his men asked if they might 'remove the heads of, at least,
one or two hundred' to teach the others a lesson, but the King
refused. The commons had spared his life when he was utterly
at their mercy and he was determined to show mercy himself.
He also ordered that the charters which he had granted at
Mile End should still be given to the men of Kent. He did this
partly because he knew that many had been forced by fear

to join the rising, partly because he knew that some were not yet satisfied. Then the great crowd of commons broke up and gradually disappeared. Some drifted away into the open country to the west and north of London. The men of Kent tramped off like driven sheep through the streets and over the river to the south. The rebels of London, now frightened men, slunk back into the dark alleys and corners of the city.

It had been a long and exhausting day, but Richard had still one more thing to do. He ordered William Walworth to put a bascinet (a light helmet) on his head because of what was going to happen. Walworth asked why he must do this.

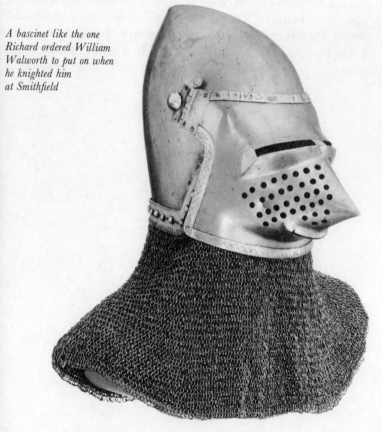

A bascinet like the one Richard ordered William Walworth to put on when he knighted him at Smithfield

Then the King told him he was 'much beholden to him' and was going to make him a knight. The Mayor answered that he was only a plain merchant who lived by trade and not worthy to be a knight, but the King made him put on the bascinet 'and strongly dubbed him knight with great good will' giving him land worth £100. He also knighted three other London citizens and gave each of them lands worth £40. Then the King rode back to the Wardrobe 'to ease him of his toils'. After all, he was still only fourteen and although he was 'in great joy' he must have been very tired.

'Ah, fair son,' said his mother when she saw him, 'what pain and sorrow I have suffered for you this day.' Richard answered, 'Certainly, madam, I know it well, but now rejoice and thank God. I have this day recovered mine heritage, and the realm of England, which I had near lost.' It was a great moment for him.

7 Surrender at St Albans

That night London was almost quiet again after the turmoil of the last three days. You can imagine how thankful people were to be able to sleep peacefully once more, whether their beds were soft feather ones, or simply rough sacks filled with prickly straw. Only a few stray rebels still shouted in the streets, and some fires still smouldered. Sir William Walworth now had a band of armed citizens on the alert to guard the city, and he also had power to punish anyone found breaking the peace. Soon after the King got back to the Wardrobe from Smithfield he had appointed Walworth and four other well-known citizens 'to keep, defend, protect, and rule the said city...and to punish everyone who makes riots and risings against our peace; either according to the law of our kingdom OR BY OTHER WAYS. The last four words meant that people could be punished without trial by beheading or mutilation, that is cutting off limbs: fingers and toes, or a leg, an arm, or ears. These horrible punishments were not used a great deal, but some rioters, who went on stealing and burning on Saturday night, and were caught in the act, were executed on the spot. The rest vanished into the darkness, out of London, or into the back streets.

Wat Tyler was dead, John Ball had disappeared after Smithfield and the King was no longer helpless. Within three days, hundreds of well-armed knights and gentlemen from all over the country flocked into London and gathered round him. He now had an army at his back and each day he inspected it at Blackheath, the very place where the rebels had camped only a week before. Richard rode through their ranks on a great war-horse, with the royal standard carried before him, and enjoyed himself very much. It was a pleasant change to be cheered by all these loyal knights and gentlemen and greeted as their sovereign lord, instead of riding among dirty rebels, not too sure of his safety.

The revolt in London was quite over and you might have expected it to collapse everywhere, but this did not happen at once. The infection had spread and in spite of Wat Tyler's death there was still rioting in many parts of Essex and Kent, in a dozen places round London, and further away in Cambridge, Norwich, Worcester and York. Rebel bands at first refused to give in. They still went about 'in malice and evil to spoil the land and destroy good men'.

One sharp outburst was at St Albans about 30 kilometres north of London. In 1381 this was a small town which had grown up round the *abbey* of St Albans where Thomas Walsingham wrote his chronicle. He was an eye-witness of what happened, and of course was horrified and angry. You can imagine him groaning aloud to himself as he wrote 'Dies irae et miserae' – 'Oh day of wrath and misery'.

St Albans Abbey was very rich, with much land and many tenants, and the monks clung to all their ancient rights. Their tenants were still villeins, whether they worked on the abbey lands or as craftsmen in the little town. All were forced to give service and pay dues. For years there had been constant trouble, the tenants struggling for freedom, the Abbot determined not to give it. Of course when the news came of the risings in Essex and Kent and the march on London, the abbey tenants decided to join in. A chosen band went to London on Friday 14 June and joined the crowds at Mile End when the King rode out there from the Tower. They were led by three men. Two were abbey tenants, William Cadyndon the town baker, and Richard of Wallingford, the most important villein. The third, William Grindcob, was the most interesting, for he had been brought up and educated in the *monastery* and was related to some of the monks there. Walsingham saw him as a dreadful traitor because he had refused to become

Villeins before the Lord's steward. They look quiet and respectful in the picture, but are quite likely complaining about their services, or demanding their freedom

a monk and had left the monastery. He calls him a fool and a worker of malice, but Grindcob must have been a brave man to give up the security of the monastery, and risk the danger of *excommunication*, which was a terrible thing in those days.

At Mile End the crowd was so great that it was difficult for the men from St Albans to get near the King. William Grindcob had to kneel on the ground six times before he managed to speak to him and tell him what they wanted, which was their freedom from serfdom. He begged the King to send a letter to

73

the Abbot ordering him to grant their demands. Richard, as you know, was ready that day to promise anything to appease the rebels and he answered that a royal letter would be ready next morning. Richard of Wallingford was chosen to wait for it, while the rest hurried off to find Wat Tyler and get him on their side too, for some thought he was more powerful than the King. He promised to come to St Albans himself if necessary, at the head of 40,000 men and he swore his usual oath to 'shave the beards' of the Abbot and monks. He did neither of these things for by the next evening he was dead.

After seeing Wat Tyler the men of St Albans set off for home, full of cheer. When they got there, without waiting for the royal letter, they told all their friends that the King had abolished the rights of the Abbot over them and they were free men. Although they had had a hard day and had walked about 60 kilometres, they wanted to show their new freedom before they went to bed, so they broke down some gates into the Abbot's wood, and tore down some of his sheep-folds, and burnt a house belonging to the monastery. 'These fools', wrote Walsingham, 'proved themselves completely mad by spending the whole night before they went to rest, breaking down folds, destroying gates and over-turning the said house. Thus ended Friday at St Albans with its train of evil.'

Early next morning Richard of Wallingford arrived with the King's letter, went into the abbey and demanded to see the Abbot. He would have preferred to die rather than give in, but the monks begged him to save the abbey and he went down to meet the rebels 'like a beaten man'. He was given the letter to read. 'Very dear in God,' it said, 'We will and command that you deliver to the good people of the town certain charters that you hold.' These charters were the abbey records of all the tenants and the services and dues they owed. After a long discussion the Abbot handed over the charters. The 'good people of the town' joyfully burnt them in the market place. Then, feeling that they were no longer slaves but masters, they defiantly drained the Abbot's fish-ponds, broke down more gates and hedges, and hung a dead rabbit on a pole to show that they could now hunt wherever they liked. All this, wrote Walsingham, they did with a 'devilish shouting and hooting which they had learned in London'. Some of them went into the monastery and tore up some round stones from the floor of a room. This may seem an odd thing to do, but the stones were famous in St Albans for they were old mill-stones put there by a former abbot who wanted to stop his tenants from building their own mills and make them use his (and of course pay for the use). He had simply seized their grind-stones and paved his private parlour with them. Now the tenants broke them up, handed them round 'like holy bread in a parish church' and kept little bits of them in their pockets for luck.

All this was very exciting to the people of St Albans, but soon the news of Wat Tyler's death arrived and they became much more cautious. They stopped destroying abbey property and drew up a new charter for the Abbot to sign. It was a simple one and not very violent. He was to:

1. Abolish serfdom.
2. Give the tenants the right to feed their animals on waste land and to hunt and fish in his woods and ponds, and set up their own mills.
3. Allow those who lived in the town to govern themselves without interference from the monks.

The Abbot agreed to these demands. He was a wise man and he, too, now knew of Wat Tyler's death, and must have expected that things would soon change again, and he would then be able to tear up the new charter and go back to the old ways.

For the time being the men of St Albans had got the better of the Abbot, but it was not for long. By now the King and his Council had recovered their wits and had begun to crush the remaining rebels. On 12 July Richard himself arrived with his army at St Albans. While he was there John Ball was brought to the town to be tried before the Chief *Justice*. He had been found hiding in a ruined house in Coventry. Now he freely admitted that he had helped to lead the rebels, and had written those mysterious letters which went round the land. He could have begged the King for pardon but he refused to do so, and was condemned to be hung, drawn, and quartered. The horrible punishment was carried out in public and before the King. The people of St Albans shook in their shoes.

Then the whole town was ordered to gather in the abbey courtyard. There they knelt humbly down and confessed their guilt in rebelling against the King, and the Abbot. They swore never to rise in arms again. They gave up their new charter to the Abbot and promised to pay £200 for all the damage they had done. But this was not the end of the matter. After Richard had gone, eighty people in St Albans and the country nearby were arrested and fifteen were executed. William Grindcob was one of them. While he was still free, but knew that he was almost certain to die, he made a short farewell speech to the people of St Albans:

> 'Fellow citizens, who have now had a little liberty after long years of oppression, stand firm while you can, and do not be afraid because of my persecution. If it should happen that I die in the cause of liberty, I will count myself happy to end my life as such a martyr.'

The words show William to be one of the best of the leaders of the revolt, a man without fear for his own life, a man without greed for power, who only wanted to help the poor and downtrodden.

8 Rebellion Crushed

As the people of St Albans anxiously watched Richard in the abbey courtyard some of them must have wondered at the change in him. Was this really the same boy who had listened to them at Mile End and willingly given them the letter to the Abbot? Here was a young king who was certainly not ready to listen, or help – a much harder person altogether. He had already sent his royal officials into Kent to hunt down the remaining rebels there, and his justices to try those that were caught. Some of those found guilty of rebellion, robbery, or murder were sent to London to be punished, some were executed in Kentish towns and villages. At the sight of their dead bodies hanging by the roadside in chains 'the land grew silent and the people trembled'.

Now here was the King himself leading his army into Essex where the trouble had started. Even before he got to St Albans he had issued two proclamations which made many more people tremble. The first one said that he had no sympathy with any rebels and ordered 'all true men to resist, arrest and punish' any person found carrying weapons or breaking the peace. When news of this got around a good many rusty swords and bows and arrows must have been hastily thrown away or hidden. Next he sent a group of Essex men away with harsh words when they went to ask him to keep the promises he had made at Mile End. Those promises, he said, had been forced from him and counted for nothing. 'Oh you wretched men, detestable on land and sea, give this message to your companions: "Villeins ye are still, and villeins ye shall remain".' This was a most unpleasant surprise for anyone who had been at Mile End, or at Smithfield, and had heard the same boy say 'I will be your chief and your captain, and ye shall have all from me that ye seek'.

What happened next was even worse. On 2 July the King issued a second proclamation saying that 'by the advice of his council' he had revoked (that means taken back) all his letters granting freedom and pardon 'which had been granted in haste to the rebels'. In other words his promises were broken, and the charters and letters he had given were worthless. Walsingham says with glee that the proclamation 'comforted those faithful to the King, but alarmed the wicked'. It also alarmed many poor folk who were not at all wicked but had joined in the revolt in the hope of a better life for themselves and their families, or because they were threatened with death if they did not do so.

It seems surprising that Richard should have changed his mind so quickly, but one reason was that his ministers had now recovered themselves and taken control again. He was no longer free to do as he liked but had to take 'the advice of his council'. The lords and gentlemen of England had got over their panic and confusion. They were now beginning 'to breathe like lords' again. The King must do as they advised, and they wanted to crush the remaining rebels as soon as possible. This did not turn out to be very difficult. None of the mobs were as large or terrifying as the ones in London had been, and it was soon clear that well-armed soldiers could beat them quickly. For instance, one large crowd of rebels who had settled themselves in a camp at Billericay, behind stakes, ditches and a string of carts chained together, were easily conquered by just ten horsemen from the King's army. Five hundred of them were killed or captured and the rest scrambled over their own defences and hid in the woods.

Another outbreak in Norfolk might have been very dangerous but that too was crushed by the prompt action of one tough and fearless man. This outbreak was led by a dyer called Geoffrey Litster, who for one short glorious week ruled 78 in Norwich like a king. He and his followers had forced the

Mayor and Council to open the gates of the town and then behaved as badly as the London mobs had. Helped by a discontented crowd inside, they terrified honest citizens by their robbing and burning. Litster himself lived in the castle in almost royal state. He dined in public, waited on by four captive knights, one of whom had to cut up his meat, taste it, in case it was poisoned, and offer it to him on bended knee. His followers were delighted with this splendid sight. They called him 'King of the Commons' and cheered loudly.

'King' Geoffrey decided that it would be wise to send messengers to King Richard asking for a royal pardon for the misdeeds of his men, and for a special charter appointing him to rule in Norfolk. He chose three of his followers to go, Master Skeet, Master Trunch and Master Kybett, and two of the captive knights. To make the King look on them with favour he also sent a large sum of money, screwed out of the unhappy people of Norwich. But his messengers had only gone about 40 kilometres from Norwich when their journey ended abruptly. They were stopped in the road by a tall knight in full armour and eight armed servants, and asked who they were and what they were doing.

This knight was none other than the Bishop of Norwich, Lord Henry Despenser. He belonged to a family well known for its tough fighting men and had himself fought in Italy with one of his brothers. As soon as he heard of Geoffrey Litster's rising he gladly put on his armour once more. Wearing an iron helmet and a solid iron breast plate and carrying a sharp two-edged sword he set out with a few servants to find the rebels. When he had listened to what the two knights had to say – and they were only too pleased to explain the reasons for their journey – he at once executed Skeet, Trunch and Kybett by the roadside, sent their heads to Newmarket to be stuck up on the town gate, and then hurried on towards Norwich. As he went he was joined by many knights and gentlemen who, up to now, had lain low for fear of the commons. When they saw their bishop in full armour and waving a sword they quickly armed themselves too and followed him. 79

The Bishop soon found 'King Geoffrey' and his followers in another fortified camp. Without delay he leapt over the ditch and burst through the stockade, followed by his knights, and laid about him with his great sword. The fight was furious but short. Litster was captured and his men fled. The Bishop promptly tried him, found him guilty of rebelling against the King and condemned him to death. Before the sentence was carried out he changed his armour for priest's clothes, heard Geoffrey's confession and forgave his sins. Then he walked beside him to the block, saying prayers for his soul. After this the warlike Bishop, whenever he heard of other rebels, went to meet them at once. Sparing no one he crushed them, sending some to death and others to prison.

Gradually other risings like this were crushed, rebels were rounded up and the work of punishment began. Many, of course, had been caught redhanded and these were the first to be tried by the King's justices. Others were betrayed by their neighbours, for it was natural, though nasty, that people who feared for their own skins were ready to betray others. For instance, some Essex men, who realised the danger they were in, went to the King 'in supplication'. This time they did not ask for charters or letters. They knelt before Richard 'with bare feet and uncovered heads' and humbly begged for mercy. It was granted, but only on condition that they brought to the King the names of the most important leaders and ill-doers. The chronicle says: 'So this was done and many were delivered into custody and tried.' In that place nineteen were hung, and twelve others perished more unpleasantly by hanging, drawing and quartering, according to the brutal custom of the time. Of course some innocent men were falsely accused by their enemies from sheer spite, but on the whole justices tried to be fair, even though they themselves and other lawyers had often suffered in the revolt. Probably only about 1,500 people were executed or hanged out of the thousands that had rebelled, and at every trial the judges made twenty-four men swear to speak the truth before the court so that 'no one was spared by favour, or persecuted because of hatred'.

The justices were kept busy through July and August but at the end of August all arrests and executions were stopped by the King's order. Anyone caught making trouble after that was taken to London and tried there, but not many, for it was very expensive.

Let us now go back to the place where the revolt started, Fobbing, and see how it ended for the people there. In the records of punishments for Essex rebels there are the names of eight men from Fobbing, and beside the names are written their punishments. Here they are:

William Gildeborn	hung, 5 July 1381; his goods seized, among them seventy-four sheep
Thomas Gildeborn, his son	a fugitive
Richard Frannceys	hung; his goods seized, among them a cottage
John Wolk	hung; his goods seized
John Devin	his goods seized

The fate of some of the rebels

Ralph White	his goods seized
Richard Tripat	a fugitive
Robert Knyght	a fugitive; his goods seized, among them a boat with all its gear [that means sails, oars and ropes]

There may well have been other Fobbing men who lost their lives because of the rebellion besides William Gildeborn, Richard Frannceys and John Wolk, men who were killed in rioting, or later by the King's soldiers. We do not know, but eight is a large enough number out of a very small village to be severely punished, and even if a man's life was spared, it was a terrible thing to lose all his belongings, which could mean his bits of furniture, his tools, and his animals. One can just imagine his wife's feelings if she lost all the beds, and cooking pots, and wooden stools. This sad little list of names and punishments makes us ask several questions. How did John Devin and Ralph White and Robert Knyght manage to earn

Robert Knyght's boat, seized from him as a punishment after the rebellion, would have had sails and paddles like these. It would have been very valuable

a living when they had lost everything? Did Robert ever manage to get another boat? Did young Thomas Gildeborn and Richard Tripat ever dare to come out of hiding, and slip back to live in Fobbing again? We can never be sure of the answers to these questions. We can only try from what we know to work out what might have happened. Perhaps they managed to hide a few of their belongings before the King's officials came, and cautiously brought them out again later. Perhaps kindly relations and neighbours came to the rescue. Perhaps the Abbess of Barking Abbey, the Lady Maud Montague, who owned all the land round Fobbing, helped them. The abbey would certainly not want to lose its profits from the land there, and may well have given them tools and animals. If they did, you may be sure they first pointed out how wicked the men of Fobbing had been to take part in the revolt.

9 The End of It All

On 3 November 1381 the King called Parliament to meet in his palace of Westminster. It was almost exactly a year since the members had fought their way through storms and floods to meet at Northampton. Then they had agreed to the poll tax. Now they came to discuss the trouble it had caused. The danger was over, the 'great mischief and rebellion' had been put down. Had it done anything to help the people who took part in it; men who simply could not pay the tax, men who had to work from morning till night for very low wages, men who longed to be free from bondage? Or was it a complete failure? If you had sat in the Great Hall at Westminster listening to what the members of Parliament said, you would probably have answered 'No' to the first question and 'Yes' to the second.

The members were either nobles and bishops (the Lords) or country gentlemen and prosperous townsmen (the Commons) and these Commons were all solid and wealthy men, very different from the 'mean commons' who had tried to make their voices heard in the revolt, and very unsympathetic towards them.

Parliament first had to listen to a sermon from the new Archbishop of Canterbury. One chronicler says it was 'a good sermon preached in English'. He mentions this specially because important sermons were usually either in Latin or French. Perhaps the Archbishop guessed that some of the members might not have had much schooling and wanted to make sure they understood what he said. Then the new Treasurer of England explained why the King had called them.

The Great Hall at Westminster where Parliament met in 1381

The King [he said] specially wishes to make good *ordinances* for the return of his realm to peace and quiet after the great turmoil in certain parts... because of the rising of certain mean commons and others and their horrible misdeeds against God and the King's dignity and crown. The King wishes to provide against another rising of the same sort (which God forbid).

Then the Treasurer told them what Richard had done at Mile End and Smithfield. He had granted charters promising freedom to the rebels, and a royal pardon for their misdeeds. He had done this 'for the best, to put an end to clamour and malice for he did not then enjoy his rightful power as King'. Later he had revoked the charters. Was this what Parliament wanted? Or did they want to grant freedom to all men? There was no doubt about the answers. With one voice Parliament declared that the King had done well to revoke his promises. Villeins, they said, could not be freed without consent of Parliament and they would never agree to it 'even

85

if it were their dying day'. This was a final 'No' to the chief demand of the rebels, an end to their greatest hope.

Even if the King had wanted to keep his promises he could not do it now. He was helpless against the advice of his Council and the whole strength of Parliament, and they were not going to give up the smallest bit of their rights over their villeins. Richard had shown great courage at a time when older and wiser men had dithered and done nothing, but he was no longer his own master. In fact among the 'good ordinances' to which Parliament agreed was one which gave the King two new guardians, two noble knights who were to swear never to leave him but to be by his side wherever he went 'to govern and counsel' him. He was to be kept in order and not allowed to do anything rash. The charters he had given were collected up and 'torn and broken' before the people. The King would not, or could not, help to 'amend' their lives.

Did the rebels gain anything from Parliament at all? Rather surprisingly they gained a pardon for their rebellion. You might have expected that an angry Parliament would have hunted and persecuted them as much as possible but instead 'grace and pardon' was passed for two kinds of people. The first were those, like the fiery Bishop of Norwich, who had killed rebels instantly when they caught them, without a proper trial. If they had done this when 'resisting rioters and traitors' they were to be forgiven. The second grace and pardon was granted to 'all evil people who had risen in the disturbance and for the treason and felony they had done'. The pardon meant that some rebels were let out of prison, and all those who had fled, like Thomas Gildeborn and Robert Tripat, were safe to come out of hiding and go home. There may have been some lords who gave their villeins a bad time out of sheer malice, but on the whole the rebels were treated with mercy after this.

One clear result of the rising was that Parliament never again agreed to a poll tax. No one wanted, no one dared, to risk another 'great mischief', and as time went on the government found better ways of raising money for the safety of the kingdom and the keeping of the sea.

A woman warming her feet by the fire. She has no stockings and her boots are clumsy and home-made. She is a typical peasant woman, perhaps wondering if the rebellion was worthwhile

But the thing the rebels wanted most, their freedom, they did not get. The lords had had a great shock in those summer months of 1381, but they were too strong and solid to be made to change their ways quickly and completely. Services and dues were not suddenly abolished, and villeins were not freed, they were still treated more as goods and chattels than as human beings. But, as you have already found in chapter 3, things had already begun to change. Years before 1381 lords were finding it more profitable to free their villeins, to take money rent for land instead of services and dues, and they went on doing it more and more till there were no villeins left in England. But it was a very slow business. The Peasants' Revolt did not bring freedom to every man, it only hurried up what was already happening.

To see how slowly the change came read this letter copied into the records kept by the monks of Peterborough:

> Richard, by divine permission, Abbot of the monastery of Peterborough, to all who shall inspect this letter. Let it be known that we have caused to be free for ever William Clopton our bondman with all his brood begotten and to be begotten [that means all the children he had already and any others that might be born] and that neither we, nor any of our servants shall demand any rights over him.

The date of this letter is 1449. Perhaps William's grandfather had taken part in the Peasants' Revolt and struggled to be free more than sixty years before. The villeins of Peterborough, like many others, had to wait a very long time before they were free men.

How Do We Know?

First we must look closely at what people, including Jean Froissart, wrote down about the Peasants' Revolt at the time and soon afterwards – the chronicles. Froissart, as you know, was a chronicler and so was Thomas Walsingham. Many chroniclers were monks. Thomas Walsingham worked in the scriptorium of St Albans Abbey, another wrote at Evesham Abbey, another at Worcester, and another at St Mary-in-the-Meadows at Leicester. A chronicle which comes from St Mary's Abbey at York must have been put together by more than one person, for it is in three different handwritings. It is not written in Latin but in a mixture of bad French and English; but it is so detailed and exact that the writers must either have been eye-witnesses or have got their facts from some people who were on the spot and saw everything.

Secondly, as well as chronicles we can read poems, songs, and short rhymes which help to fill in the background. One long poem called 'The Vision of Piers Plowman' is by William Langland, a priest who was also a fine poet. He was educated at the priory of Great Malvern in Worcestershire, and loved to wander on the Malvern hills and down into the fields and villages below them. Indeed he spent most of his life wandering, sometimes taking a few church services and always writing poetry. In 'Piers Plowman' he describes some of the people he met on his travels: courtiers, lawyers, clergy, pilgrims, minstrels and merchants and the poor folk of town and country.

Many of the poems, or bits of them, must have travelled all over England, passed on from person to person by word of mouth. If you can't read (and in 1381 few people could) you can often learn a rhyme, or a chorus, or a jingle, by heart and pass it on. Some of the rhymes were very short everyday jokes like:

> Tho' pepere be blak,
> It hath a good *snak*.

Some were bitter reminders of punishment:

> The ax was sharpe, the blok was hard,
> In the fourth yeare of King Richard.

Others were used to pass on mysterious messages among the rebels and to warn them to be on the alert (chapter 3).

Thirdly there are the statements made in the law courts after the revolt had failed, when men who had taken part had been rounded up and were being tried for their lives. Eye-witnesses told the judges what they had seen and heard, and the captured rebels either defended themselves or confessed. One confession came from a man who had led some of the mobs in London. He said: 'It no longer serves me to speak falsehoods, so I will speak without any attempt to deceive.' He then told of the plans they had made, including one to take the young King prisoner.

These are some of the *sources* from which we have to dig out our information about the Peasants' Revolt and you will find extracts from them in this book. You will know these extracts because they are always put in inverted commas, like this: 'It no longer serves me'. If there are words you do not understand, or do not recognise because they are oddly spelt, like 'ympe', look them up in the list of words (the glossary).

Opposite: *Froissart presenting one of his books to Richard II. Notice the clothes*

Things to Do

1. Make a family tree of the royal family of England from Henry III to the death of Richard III. Show Richard II in a different colour. Try to put in as many people as possible.
2. Write short life stories of Edward III and Edward the Black Prince.
3. Find a copy of Chaucer's *Canterbury Tales* in modern English and read the part about the Knight. Write out a list of all the things a knight was supposed to be.
4. Find some books about how people dressed in Richard II's time. Either on your own or in a group, make pictures to show the dress of a peasant and his wife, a priest or a monk, a king, a knight, a merchant and a fine lady.
5. Draw up a list of things that people were grumbling about in Richard II's reign.
6. Write a short play about what happened at Fobbing when the tax-collector (Thomas Bampton) arrived there in 1381. You might tape-record it with sound effects.
7. Draw up a list of all the reasons you can find for the revolt of 1381, including the ones mentioned in chapter 1. Write the best on a large piece of paper as if it was a poster, making each reason clear and short.
8. Pretend to be a peasant living in Little Cornard, Essex. Describe and name your wife and family, and say what life was like in 1381.
9. Make a large map of the south-east of England, and mark on it the places mentioned in the book.
10. Describe a day's march of the rebels on the way from Canterbury to London.
11. Pretend to be John Ball and make a speech to the rebels at Blackheath on the evening of 13 June 1381.
12. Make a large map of London in 1381 and mark on it as many of the places mentioned in chapter 5 as you can. Then draw

pictures of these, or of something that happened there, and place them round the map. Link them to the places by string or coloured wool, or a coloured arrow.

13. How do you think the rebels got into London? Discuss this with your group.

14. Pretend there was radio and TV in 1381, and you are in charge of outside broadcasting. Send reporters and camera men to tape-record and film what happened in and around London on 13 and 14 June. Then prepare a news bulletin, or a TV broadcast using your material.

15. You are a guard at the Tower. Describe what happened there on 14 June.

16. Act a play about what happened in London on 15 June. Use as many people in the class as possible and divide them into the rebels, the King and his followers, and the armed men that the Mayor called out.

17. You are writing a novel about the Peasants' Revolt. Write the chapter about 15 June making Richard II your hero.

18. Try to find out whether there were any revolts in 1381 in your area. (Ask for books on local history at your public library.) If you find there were, write an account of them.

19. Imagine you are an abbey tenant of St Albans. Write an account of your visit to London led by William Grindcob. What did you do when you got home that night?

20. Imagine you are Thomas Gildeborn of Fobbing in Essex. Tell what happened to you from 4 July 1381 – June 1382.

21. What do you think of the way Richard II dealt with the rebels in July and August 1381? Hold a debate in your class for and against him and his ministers. Try to show in your speeches why Richard acted as he did. Take a vote to see who supports him.

22. What sort of people sat in Parliament in 1381. How were they chosen?

23. Draw up a list of what Parliament granted and did not grant to people who had taken part in the revolt.

24. Was the Peasants' Revolt a failure? Try to find out how long people had to wait to get their freedom in England.

Glossary

abashed, ashamed

abbey, home of monks or nuns, headed by an abbot or abbess

affrayed, frightened

aland, on land

alderman, member of town council next to the mayor in importance

allegiance, loyalty

amend, make better

appease, calm down, soothe

apprentice, someone learning a trade or craft

bogey, evil spirit or devil

bondage, slavery, villeins were in bondage

brood, children

bushel, measure of corn or fruit

calamity, dreadful happening

charter, written record of rights promised

chattels, movable belongings

chronicle, history book, often written by a monk called a chronicler

cobbles, round stones

commons, ordinary people, not nobles

craftily, skilfully

creek, little stream running into a river

crozier, special staff belonging to a bishop

document, written record

excommunication, being cut off from the Church

felony, crime, usually violent

groat, small silver coin

gyle, deceit or dishonesty

hodden, rough woollen cloth, usually grey

hull, remove the outer covering of a seed or fruit

husk, dry, outer covering of some seeds and fruit

journeyman, someone who works by, the day for a master

justice, judge

litter, 1. a kind of bed carried by men or horses; 2. rubbish

lithe, able to move his body easily

loot, something seized and carried off

malice, ill-will

mantle, long coat or cloak

meddle, mix

mitre, hat worn by a bishop

monastery, home of monks

ordinances, laws or official orders

outrageous, violent, or impossible

pilgrimage, journey to a holy place

Plantagenet, surname of kings of England from Henry II to Richard III

potage, thick soup

pottel, jug or bottle holding about 4.5 litres

proclamation, public announcement

rampage, rush about wildly

renyshe, Rhenish, made near the river Rhine in Germany

rustics, country people

scriptorium, writing room in a monastery

sergeant-at-arms, armed guard

snak, taste

solitée, a special kind of pudding

source, place where something begins

standard, flag

steward, someone who looks after his lord's lands and business

tabard, sleeveless coat worn over armour

tiler, someone who makes tiles and puts them on roofs

trespass, a misdeed, or an act against the law

undone, ruined

victuals, food and drink

villein, someone who has to give service and dues for his land and who is not free (in bondage)

wattle and daub, framework of twigs with mud or clay plastered over them

wharves, landing place where ships can tie up

winnow, shake out the outer covering of a seed or fruit

ympe, young boy

Index